GENERAL CONFERENCE ADDRESSES

GENERAL CONFERENCE ADDRESSES

JOURNAL EDITION
APRIL 2020

SALT LAKE CITY, UTAH

Book design © Deseret Book Company
Cover photo: dugdax/Shutterstock Images.
Interior photos: pages 1 and 119, KPG_Payless; page 44, Piotr Krzeslak; page 81, IgorZh/Shutterstock Images; page 153, shaifulzamri/Getty Images.

April 2020 General Conference Addresses, Journal Edition by Deseret Book Company © By Intellectual Reserve, Inc.

All rights reserved. No part of this book may be reproduced in any form or by any means without permission in writing from the publisher, Deseret Book Company, at permissions@deseretbook.com or PO Box 30178, Salt Lake City, Utah 84130.

This product, offered by Deseret Book Company, is neither made nor endorsed by Intellectual Reserve, Inc., or The Church of Jesus Christ of Latter-day Saints.

Visit us at deseretbook.com

ISBN 978-1-62972-807-0

Printed in the United States of America

10 9 8 7 6 5 4 3 2 1

CONTENTS

SATURDAY MORNING SESSION

Opening Message 2
PRESIDENT RUSSELL M. NELSON

Shall We Not Go On in So Great a Cause? 5
PRESIDENT M. RUSSELL BALLARD

Ensuring a Righteous Judgment 12
ELDER JAMES R. RASBAND

An Especially Noble Calling 18
JOY D. JONES

Spiritually Defining Memories 24
ELDER NEIL L. ANDERSEN

Deep in Our Heart 31
DOUGLAS D. HOLMES

Prayers of Faith 38
PRESIDENT HENRY B. EYRING

SATURDAY AFTERNOON SESSION

The Coming Forth of the Book of Mormon 45
ELDER ULISSES SOARES

Come unto Christ—
Living as Latter-day Saints 52
ELDER JOHN A. McCUNE

CONTENTS

A Living Witness of the Living Christ 57
BISHOP GÉRALD CAUSSÉ

Consider the Goodness and Greatness of God 62
ELDER DALE G. RENLUND

The Power of the Book of Mormon in Conversion 69
ELDER BENJAMIN M. Z. TAI

A Good Foundation against the Time to Come 74
ELDER GARY E. STEVENSON

SATURDAY EVENING SESSION

Hosanna and Hallelujah—The Living Jesus Christ: The Heart
of Restoration and Easter 82
ELDER GERRIT W. GONG

How the Priesthood Blesses Youth 89
LAUDY RUTH KAOUK

How the Priesthood Blesses Youth 92
ENZO SERGE PETELO

United in Accomplishing God's Work 96
JEAN B. BINGHAM

He Goes before Us 103
PRESIDENT HENRY B. EYRING

The Melchizedek Priesthood and the Keys 109
PRESIDENT DALLIN H. OAKS

Opening the Heavens for Help 115
PRESIDENT RUSSELL M. NELSON

SUNDAY MORNING SESSION

Fulfillment of Prophecy 120
ELDER RONALD A. RASBAND

CONTENTS

That They May See 126
BONNIE H. CORDON

A Perfect Brightness of Hope 131
ELDER JEFFREY R. HOLLAND

"Let This House Be Built unto My Name" 137
ELDER DAVID A. BEDNAR

Hear Him 144
PRESIDENT RUSSELL M. NELSON

Hosanna Shout 152
PRESENTED BY PRESIDENT RUSSELL M. NELSON

SUNDAY AFTERNOON SESSION

The Great Plan 154
PRESIDENT DALLIN H. OAKS

The Blessing of Continuing Revelation to Prophets and Personal Revelation to Guide Our Lives 160
ELDER QUENTIN L. COOK

Finding Refuge from the Storms of Life 168
ELDER RICARDO P. GIMÉNEZ

Come and Belong 173
ELDER DIETER F. UCHTDORF

The Finest Homes 180
ELDER L. WHITNEY CLAYTON

Sharing the Message of the Restoration and the Resurrection 185
ELDER D. TODD CHRISTOFFERSON

Go Forward in Faith 191
PRESIDENT RUSSELL M. NELSON

Saturday Morning Session

April 4, 2020

OPENING MESSAGE
PRESIDENT RUSSELL M. NELSON
President of The Church of Jesus Christ of Latter-day Saints

My beloved brothers and sisters, as we welcome you to this historic April 2020 general conference of The Church of Jesus Christ of Latter-day Saints, for reasons you know, I stand before you in an empty auditorium!

Little did I know, when I promised you at the October 2019 general conference that this April conference would be "memorable" and "unforgettable," that speaking to a visible congregation of fewer than 10 people would make this conference so memorable and unforgettable *for me!* Yet the knowledge that you are participating by electronic transmission, and the choir's beautiful rendition of "It Is Well with My Soul," bring great comfort to *my* soul.

As you know, attendance at this general conference has been strictly limited as part of our efforts to be good global citizens and do all we can to limit the spread of COVID-19. This virus has had a major impact throughout the world. It has also altered our Church meetings, missionary service, and temple work for a while.

Though today's restrictions relate to a virulent virus, life's personal trials stretch far beyond this pandemic. Future trials could result from an accident, a natural disaster, or an unexpected personal heartache.

How can we endure such trials? The Lord has told us that "if ye are prepared ye shall not fear" (Doctrine and Covenants 38:30). Of course, we can store our own reserves of food, water, and savings. But equally crucial is our need to fill our personal *spiritual* storehouses with faith, truth, and testimony.

Our ultimate quest in life is to prepare to meet our Maker. We do this by striving daily to become more like our Savior, Jesus Christ (see 3 Nephi 27:27). And we do *that* as we repent daily and receive His cleansing, healing, and strengthening power. Then we can feel enduring peace and joy, even during turbulent times. This is exactly why the Lord has implored us to stand in holy places and "be not moved" (Doctrine and Covenants 87:8).

This year, we commemorate the 200th anniversary of one of the most significant events in the history of the world—namely, the appearance of God the Father and His Beloved Son, Jesus Christ, to Joseph Smith. During that singular vision, God the Father pointed to Jesus Christ and said: "This is My Beloved Son. Hear Him!" (Joseph Smith—History 1:17).

That admonition given to Joseph is for each of us. We are to seek, in every way we can, to hear Jesus Christ, who speaks to us through the power and ministering of the Holy Ghost.

The purpose of this and every general conference is to help us to hear Him. We have prayed, and invite you to pray, that the Spirit of the Lord will be with us in such rich abundance that you can hear the messages that the Savior has especially for you—messages that will bring peace to your soul. Messages that will heal your broken heart. Messages that will illuminate your mind. Messages that will help you know what to do as you move ahead through times of turmoil and trial.

We pray that this conference will be memorable and unforgettable because of the messages you will hear, the unique announcements which will be made, and the experiences in which you will be invited to participate.

For example, at the conclusion of the Sunday morning session, we will convene a worldwide solemn assembly when I will lead you in the sacred Hosanna Shout. We pray that this will be a spiritual highlight for you as we express in global unison our profound gratitude to God the Father and His Beloved Son by praising Them in this unique way.

For this sacred experience, we use clean white handkerchiefs. But if you do not have one, you may simply wave your hand. At the conclusion of the Hosanna Shout, the congregation will join with the choir in singing "The Spirit of God" (*Hymns,* no. 2).

My dear brothers and sisters, this conference will be magnificent. This year will be extraordinary as we focus intently on the

Savior and His restored gospel. The most important lasting effects of this historic conference will be as our hearts change and we commence a lifelong quest to hear Him.

Welcome to April 2020 general conference! I know that God, our Heavenly Father, and His Son, Jesus Christ, are mindful of us. They will be with us throughout the proceedings of these two glorious days as we seek to draw closer to Them and honor Them. In the sacred name of Jesus Christ, amen.

SHALL WE NOT GO ON IN SO GREAT A CAUSE?

PRESIDENT M. RUSSELL BALLARD
Acting President of the Quorum of the Twelve Apostles

Thank you very much, President, for such a wonderful opening. Brothers and sisters, 215 years ago, a little boy was born to Joseph and Lucy Mack Smith in Vermont in a region known as New England in the northeastern United States.

Joseph and Lucy Mack believed in Jesus Christ, studied the holy scriptures, sincerely prayed, and walked with faith in God.

They named their new baby son Joseph Smith Jr.

Of the Smith family, Brigham Young said: "The Lord had his eye upon [Joseph Smith], and upon his father, and upon his father's father, and upon their progenitors clear back to Abraham, and from Abraham to the flood, from the flood to Enoch and from Enoch to Adam. He has watched that family and that blood as it has circulated from its fountain to the birth of that man. [Joseph Smith] was foreordained in eternity."[1]

Beloved by his family, Joseph Jr. was particularly close to his older brother Hyrum, who was nearly six years of age when Joseph was born.

Last October, I sat by the hearthstone that was in the small Smith home in Sharon, Vermont, where Joseph was born. I felt Hyrum's love for Joseph and thought of him holding his baby brother in his arms and teaching him how to walk.

Father and Mother Smith experienced personal setbacks, forcing them to move their family numerous times before finally giving up on New England and making the courageous decision to move farther west, to New York State.

Because the family was united, they survived these challenges and together faced the daunting task of starting over again on a hundred-acre (0.4 km^2) wooded tract of land in Manchester, near Palmyra, New York.

I am not sure that many of us realize the physical and emotional challenges that starting over presented the Smith family—clearing land, planting orchards and fields, building a small log home and other farm structures, hiring out as day laborers, and making home goods to sell in town.

By the time the family arrived in western New York, the area was ablaze with religious fervor—known as the Second Great Awakening.

During this time of debate and strife among religious parties, Joseph experienced a wondrous vision, known today as the First Vision. We are blessed to have four primary accounts from which I will draw.[2]

Joseph recorded: "During this time of great [religious] excitement my mind was called up to serious reflection and great uneasiness; but though my feelings were deep and often poignant, still I kept myself aloof from all these parties, though I attended their several meetings as often as occasion would permit. . . . [Yet] so great were the confusion and strife among the different denominations, that it was impossible for a person young as I was, and so unacquainted with men and things, to come to any certain conclusion who was right and who was wrong."[3]

Joseph turned to the Bible to find answers to his questions and read James 1:5: "If any of you lack wisdom, let him ask of God, that giveth to all men liberally, and upbraideth not; and it shall be given him."[4]

He noted: "Never did any passage of scripture come with more power to the heart of man than this did at this time to mine. It seemed to enter with great force into every feeling of my heart. I reflected on it again and again."[5]

Joseph came to realize that the Bible did not contain all the answers to life's questions; rather, it taught men and women how they could find answers to their questions by communicating directly with God through prayer.

He added: "So, in accordance with this, my determination to ask of God, I retired to the woods to make the attempt. It was on the morning of a beautiful, clear day, early in the spring of eighteen hundred and twenty."[6]

Soon thereafter, Joseph said that "[a pillar of] light rested upon me [and] I saw two Personages, whose brightness and glory defy all description, standing above me in the air. One of them spake unto me, calling me by name and said, pointing to the other—[Joseph,] *This is My Beloved Son. Hear Him!*"[7]

The Savior then spoke: "Joseph, my son, thy sins are forgiven thee. Go thy way, walk in my statutes, and keep my commandments. Behold, I am the Lord of glory. I was crucified for the world, that all those who believe on my name may have eternal life."[8]

Joseph added, "No sooner, therefore, did I get possession of myself, so as to be able to speak, than I asked the Personages who stood above me in the light, which of all the sects was right."[9]

He recalled: "They told me that all religious denominations were believing in incorrect doctrines, and that none of them was acknowledged of God as his church and kingdom. And . . . at the same time [I] receive[d] a promise that the fulness of the gospel should at some future time be made known unto me."[10]

Joseph also noted, "I saw many angels in this vision."[11]

Following this glorious vision, Joseph wrote: "My soul was filled with love, and for many days I could rejoice with great joy. . . . The Lord was with me."[12]

He emerged from the Sacred Grove to begin his preparation to become a prophet of God.

Joseph also began to learn what ancient prophets experienced—rejection, opposition, and persecution. Joseph recalled sharing what he had seen and heard with one of the ministers who had been active in the religious revival:

"I was greatly surprised at his behavior; he treated my communication not only lightly, but with great contempt, saying it was all of the devil, that there were no such things as visions or revelations in these days; that all such things had ceased with the apostles, and that there would never be any more of them.

"I soon found, however, that my telling the story had excited a great deal of prejudice against me among professors of religion, and was the cause of great persecution, which continued to increase; . . .

and this was common among all the sects—all united to persecute me."[13]

Three years later, in 1823, the heavens opened again as part of the continuing Restoration of the gospel of Jesus Christ in the last days. Joseph noted that an angel named Moroni appeared to him and said "that God had a work for me to do . . . [and that] there was a book deposited, written upon gold plates" that contained "the fulness of the everlasting Gospel . . . as delivered by the Savior to the ancient inhabitants [of the Americas]."[14]

Eventually, Joseph obtained, translated, and published the ancient record, known today as the Book of Mormon.

His brother Hyrum, who had been his constant supporter, especially following his painful, life-threatening leg operation in 1813, was one of the witnesses of the gold plates. He was also one of the six members of the Church of Jesus Christ when it was organized in 1830.

During their lives, Joseph and Hyrum faced mobs and persecution together. For example, they languished in the most wretched conditions in the Liberty Jail in Missouri for five months during the cold winter of 1838–39.

In April 1839, Joseph wrote his wife Emma describing their situation in Liberty Jail: "I believe it is now about five months and six days since I have been under the grimace of a guard, night and day, and within the walls, grates, and screeching iron doors of a lonesome, dark, dirty prison. . . . We shall be moved from this [place] at any rate, and we are glad of it. Let what will become of us, we cannot get into a worse hole than this is. . . . We shall never cast a lingering wish after Liberty in Clay County, Missouri. We have enough of it to last forever."[15]

In the face of persecution, Hyrum exhibited faith in the Lord's promises, including a guarantee to escape his enemies if he so chose. In a blessing Hyrum received in 1835 under the hands of Joseph Smith, the Lord promised him: "Thou shalt have power to escape the hand of thine enemies. Thy life shall be sought with untiring zeal, but thou shalt escape. *If it please thee,* and thou desirest, *thou shalt have the power voluntarily to lay down thy life* to glorify God."[16]

In June 1844, Hyrum was presented the choice to live or to lay down his life to glorify God and to "seal his testimony with his blood"—side by side together with his beloved brother Joseph.[17]

A week before the fateful trip to Carthage, where they were murdered in cold blood by an armed mob of cowards who had painted their faces to avoid detection, Joseph recorded that "I advised my brother Hyrum to take his family on the next steamboat and go to Cincinnati."

I still feel great emotion as I remember Hyrum's reply: "Joseph, *I can't leave you.*"[18]

So Joseph and Hyrum went to Carthage, where they became martyrs for Christ's cause and name.

The official announcement of the martyrdom stated the following: "Joseph Smith, the Prophet and Seer of the Lord, . . . has brought forth the Book of Mormon, which he translated by the gift and power of God, and has been the means of publishing it on two continents; has sent the fulness of the everlasting gospel, which it contained, to the four quarters of the earth; has brought forth the revelations and commandments which compose this book of Doctrine and Covenants, and many other wise documents and instructions for the benefit of the children of men; gathered many thousands of the Latter-day Saints, founded a great city, and left a fame and name that cannot be slain. . . . And like most of the Lord's anointed in ancient times, [Joseph] has sealed his mission and his works with his own blood; and so has his brother Hyrum. *In life they were not divided, and in death they were not separated!*"[19]

Following the martyrdom, Joseph's and Hyrum's bodies were returned to Nauvoo, washed, and dressed so the Smith family could see their loved ones. Their precious mother recalled: "I had for a long time braced every nerve, roused every energy of my soul, and called upon God to strengthen me; but when I entered the room, and saw my murdered sons extended both at once before my eyes, and heard the sobs and groans of my family [and] the cries . . . from the lips of their wives, children, brothers, and sisters, it was too much. I sank back crying to the Lord in the agony of my soul, 'My God! My God! Why hast thou forsaken this family?'"[20]

At that moment of sorrow and distress, she recalled them saying, "Mother, weep not for us; we have overcome the world by love."[21]

They had indeed overcome the world. Joseph and Hyrum Smith, like those faithful Saints described in the book of Revelation, "came out of great tribulation, and have washed their robes, and made them white in the blood of the Lamb [and] are . . . before the throne of God, and serve him day and night in his temple: and he that sitteth on the throne shall dwell among them.

"They shall hunger no more, neither thirst any more; neither shall the sun light on them, nor any heat.

"For the Lamb which is in the midst of the throne shall feed them, and shall lead them unto living fountains of waters: and God shall wipe away all tears from their eyes."[22]

As we celebrate this joyous occasion, the 200th anniversary of the First Vision, we should always remember the price Joseph and Hyrum Smith paid, along with so many other faithful men, women, and children, to establish the Church so you and I could enjoy the many blessings and all of these revealed truths we have today. Their faithfulness should never be forgotten!

I have often wondered why Joseph and Hyrum and their families had to suffer so much. It may be that they came to know God through their suffering in ways that could not have happened without it. Through it, they reflected on Gethsemane and the cross of the Savior. As Paul said, "For unto you it is given in the behalf of Christ, not only to believe on him, but also to suffer for his sake."[23]

Before his death in 1844, Joseph wrote a spirited letter to the Saints. It was a call to action, which continues in the Church today:

"Brethren [and sisters], *shall we not go on in so great a cause?* Go forward and not backward. Courage, brethren [and sisters]; and on, on to the victory! . . .

" . . . Let us, therefore, as a church and a people, and as Latter-day Saints, offer unto the Lord an offering in righteousness."[24]

As we listen to the Spirit during this 200th anniversary celebration this weekend, consider what offering you will present to the Lord in righteousness in the coming days. Be courageous—share it with someone you trust, and most important, please take the time to do it!

I know that the Savior is pleased when we present Him an offering from our hearts in righteousness, just as He was pleased with the faithful offering of those remarkable brothers, Joseph and Hyrum Smith, and all other faithful Saints. Of this I solemnly testify in the sacred and holy name of our Lord Jesus Christ, amen.

Notes

1. Brigham Young, in *Teachings of Presidents of the Church: Joseph Smith* (2007), 544; see also Brigham Young, "Remarks," *Deseret News,* Oct. 26, 1859, 266.
2. There are four primary accounts of the First Vision from which I quote; see "Joseph Smith's Accounts of the First Vision," josephsmithpapers.org.
3. Joseph Smith—History 1:8.
4. See Joseph Smith—History 1:11.
5. Joseph Smith—History 1:12.
6. Joseph Smith—History 1:14.
7. Joseph Smith—History 1:17.
8. In Joseph Smith, "History, circa Summer 1832," 3, josephsmithpapers.org; spelling, punctuation, and capitalization standardized.
9. Joseph Smith—History 1:18.
10. Joseph Smith, "Church History," *Times and Seasons,* Mar. 1, 1842, 707; see also josephsmithpapers.org.
11. Joseph Smith, "Journal, 1835–1836," 24, josephsmithpapers.org.
12. Joseph Smith, "History, circa Summer 1832," 3, josephsmithpapers.org; punctuation and capitalization standardized.
13. Joseph Smith—History 1:21–22.
14. Joseph Smith—History 1:33–34.
15. Joseph Smith, "Letter to Emma Smith, 4 April 1839," 1–2, josephsmithpapers.org; spelling, punctuation, and capitalization standardized.
16. Joseph Smith, in "Minute Book 1," 186, josephsmithpapers.org; emphasis added; punctuation standardized.
17. See Doctrine and Covenants 136:39.
18. Joseph Smith, "History of Joseph Smith," *The Latter-day Saints' Millennial Star,* Apr. 19, 1862, 248; emphasis added.
19. Doctrine and Covenants 135:3; emphasis added.
20. "Lucy Mack Smith, History, 1845," 312–13, josephsmithpapers.org; spelling and punctuation standardized.
21. "Lucy Mack Smith, History, 1845," 313, josephsmithpapers.org.
22. Revelation 7:14–17.
23. Philippians 1:29.
24. Doctrine and Covenants 128:22, 24; emphasis added.

ENSURING A RIGHTEOUS JUDGMENT

ELDER JAMES R. RASBAND
Of the Seventy

The Book of Mormon Teaches the Doctrine of Christ

Last October, President Russell M. Nelson challenged us to consider how our lives would be different if our "knowledge gained from the Book of Mormon were suddenly taken away."[1] I have pondered on his question, as I am sure many of you have. One thought has come again and again—without the Book of Mormon and its clarity about the doctrine of Christ and His atoning sacrifice, where would I turn for peace?

The doctrine of Christ—which consists of the saving principles and ordinances of faith in Christ, repentance, baptism, the gift of the Holy Ghost, and enduring to the end—is taught numerous times in all the scriptures of the Restoration but with particular power in the Book of Mormon.[2] The doctrine begins with faith in Christ, and every one of its elements depends upon trust in His atoning sacrifice.

As President Nelson has taught, "The Book of Mormon provides the fullest and most authoritative understanding of the Atonement of Jesus Christ to be found anywhere."[3] The more we understand about the Savior's supernal gift, the more we will come to know, in our minds and in our hearts,[4] the reality of President Nelson's assurance that "the truths of the Book of Mormon have the *power* to heal, comfort, restore, succor, strengthen, console, and cheer our souls."[5]

The Savior's Atonement Satisfies All the Demands of Justice

A vital and peace-giving contribution of the Book of Mormon to our understanding of the Savior's Atonement is its teaching that Christ's merciful sacrifice fulfills all the demands of justice. As Alma explained, "God himself atoneth for the sins of the world, to bring about the plan of mercy, to appease the demands of justice, that God might be a perfect, just God, and a merciful God also."[6] The

Father's plan of mercy[7]—what the scriptures also call the plan of happiness[8] or the plan of salvation[9]—could not be accomplished unless all the demands of justice were satisfied.

But what exactly are the "demands of justice"? Consider Alma's own experience. Remember that as a young man, Alma went about seeking "to destroy the church."[10] In fact, Alma told his son Helaman that he was "tormented with the pains of hell" because he had effectively "murdered many of [God's] children" by leading "them away unto destruction."[11]

Alma explained to Helaman that peace finally came to him when his "mind caught hold" on his father's teaching "concerning the coming of . . . Jesus Christ . . . to atone for the sins of the world."[12] A penitent Alma pleaded for Christ's mercy[13] and then felt joy and relief when he realized that Christ had atoned for his sins and paid all that justice required. Again, what would justice have required of Alma? As Alma himself later taught, "No unclean thing can inherit the kingdom of God."[14] Thus, part of Alma's relief must have been that unless mercy interceded, justice would have prevented him from returning to live with Heavenly Father.[15]

The Savior Heals the Wounds We Cannot Heal

But was Alma's joy focused solely on himself—on *his* avoiding punishment and *his* being able to return to the Father? We know that Alma also agonized about those whom he had led away from the truth.[16] But Alma himself could not heal and restore all those he had led away. He could not himself ensure that they would be given a fair opportunity to learn the doctrine of Christ and to be blessed by living its joyful principles. He could not bring back those who may have died still blinded by his false teaching.

As President Boyd K. Packer once taught: "The thought that rescued Alma . . . is this: Restoring what you cannot restore, healing the wound you cannot heal, fixing that which you broke and you cannot fix is the very purpose of the atonement of Christ."[17] The joyous truth on which Alma's mind "caught hold" was not just that he himself could be made clean but also that those whom he had harmed could be healed and made whole.

The Savior's Sacrifice Ensures a Righteous Judgment

Years before Alma was rescued by this reassuring doctrine, King Benjamin had taught about the breadth of healing offered by the Savior's atoning sacrifice. King Benjamin declared that "glad tidings of great joy" were given him "by an angel from God."[18] Among those glad tidings was the truth that Christ would suffer and die for our sins and mistakes to ensure that "a *righteous judgment* might come upon the children of men."[19]

What exactly does a "righteous judgment" require? In the next verse, King Benjamin explained that to ensure a righteous judgment, the Savior's blood atoned "for the sins of those who have fallen by the transgression of Adam" and for those "who have died not knowing the will of God concerning them, or who have ignorantly sinned."[20] A righteous judgment also required, he taught, that "the blood of Christ atoneth for" the sins of little children.[21]

These scriptures teach a glorious doctrine: the Savior's atoning sacrifice heals, as a free gift, those who sin in ignorance—those to whom, as Jacob put it, "there is no law given."[22] Accountability for sin depends on the light we have been given and hinges on our ability to exercise our agency.[23] We know this healing and comforting truth only because of the Book of Mormon and other Restoration scripture.[24]

Of course, where there is a law given, where we are not ignorant of the will of God, we are accountable. As King Benjamin emphasized: "Wo unto him who knoweth that he rebelleth against God! For salvation cometh to none such except it be through repentance and faith on the Lord Jesus Christ."[25]

This too is glad tidings of the doctrine of Christ. Not only does the Savior heal and restore those who sin in ignorance, but also, for those who sin against the light, the Savior offers healing on the condition of repentance and faith in Him.[26]

Alma must have "caught hold" of both these truths. Would Alma truly have felt what he describes as "exquisite . . . joy"[27] if he thought that Christ saved him but left forever harmed those he had led away from the truth? Surely not. For Alma to feel complete peace, those he harmed also needed the opportunity to be made whole.

But how exactly would they—or those we may harm—be made whole? Although we do not fully understand the sacred mechanics by which the Savior's atoning sacrifice heals and restores, we do know that to ensure a righteous judgment, the Savior will clear away the underbrush of ignorance and the painful thorns of hurt caused by others.[28] By this He ensures that all God's children will be given the opportunity, with unobscured vision, to choose to follow Him and accept the great plan of happiness.[29]

The Savior Will Mend All That We Have Broken

It is these truths that would have brought Alma peace. And it is these truths that should bring us great peace as well. As natural men and women, we all bump, or sometimes crash, into each other and cause harm. As any parent can testify, the pain associated with our mistakes is not simply the fear of our own punishment but the fear that we may have limited our children's joy or in some way hindered them from seeing and understanding the truth. The glorious promise of the Savior's atoning sacrifice is that as far as our mistakes as parents are concerned, He holds our children blameless and promises healing for them.[30] And even when they have sinned against the light—as we all do—His arm of mercy is outstretched,[31] and He will redeem them if they will but look to Him and live.[32]

Although the Savior has power to mend what we cannot fix, He commands us to do all we can to make restitution as part of our repentance.[33] Our sins and mistakes displace not only our relationship with God but also our relationships with others. Sometimes our efforts to heal and restore may be as simple as an apology, but other times restitution may require years of humble effort.[34] Yet, for many of our sins and mistakes, we simply are not able to fully heal those we have hurt. The magnificent, peace-giving promise of the Book of Mormon and the restored gospel is that the Savior will mend all that we have broken.[35] And He will also mend us if we turn to Him in faith and repent of the harm we have caused.[36] He offers both of these gifts because He loves all of us with perfect love[37] and because He is committed to ensuring a righteous judgment that honors both justice and mercy. I testify this is true in the name of Jesus Christ, amen.

Notes

1. Russell M. Nelson, "Closing Remarks," *Ensign* or *Liahona,* Nov. 2019, 122.
2. See 2 Nephi 31; 3 Nephi 11:28, 32, 35, 39–40; Doctrine and Covenants 10:62–63, 67–70; 68:25; Moses 6:52–54; 8:24; Articles of Faith 1:4.
3. Russell M. Nelson, "The Book of Mormon: What Would Your Life Be Like without It?" *Ensign* or *Liahona,* Nov. 2017, 62.
4. See Doctrine and Covenants 8:2–3.
5. Russell M. Nelson, "The Book of Mormon: What Would Your Life Be Like without It?" 62.
6. Alma 42:15.
7. See Alma 42:15.
8. See Alma 42:8.
9. See Alma 24:14; Moses 6:62.
10. See Mosiah 27:8–10.
11. Alma 36:13, 14.
12. Alma 36:17, 18.
13. See Alma 36:18.
14. Alma 40:26; see also 1 Nephi 15:34; Alma 7:21; 11:37; Helaman 8:25.
15. See 3 Nephi 27:19; see also Moses 6:57.
16. See Alma 36:14–17.
17. Boyd K. Packer, "The Brilliant Morning of Forgiveness," *Ensign,* Nov. 1995, 19–20.
18. Mosiah 3:2, 3.
19. Mosiah 3:10; emphasis added.
20. Mosiah 3:11; see also 2 Nephi 9:26.
21. Mosiah 3:16; see also Mosiah 15:25; Moroni 8:11–12, 22.
22. 2 Nephi 9:25.
23. See 2 Nephi 2:26–27; Helaman 14:29–30.
24. See Articles of Faith 1:2; see also Doctrine and Covenants 45:54. Elaborating on the doctrine of baptism for the dead, the Prophet Joseph once said: "While one portion of the human race is judging and condemning the other without mercy, the Great Parent of the universe looks upon the whole of the human family with a fatherly care and paternal regard; He views them as His offspring. . . . He is a wise Lawgiver, and will judge all men, not according to the narrow, contracted notions of men. . . . He will judge them, 'not according to what they have not, but according to what they have'; those who have lived without law, will be judged without law, and those who have a law, will be judged by that law. We need not doubt the wisdom and intelligence of the Great Jehovah; He will award judgment or mercy to all nations according to their several deserts, their means of obtaining intelligence, the laws by which they are governed, the facilities afforded them of obtaining correct information, and . . . we shall all of us eventually have to confess that the Judge of all the earth has done right" (*Teachings of Presidents of the Church: Joseph Smith* [2007], 404).
25. Mosiah 3:12; see also 2 Nephi 9:27.
26. See Mosiah 3:12; Helaman 14:30; Moroni 8:10; Doctrine and Covenants 101:78. Individuals may be ignorant of certain commandments and covenants or be unable to exercise their agency

in some circumstances but still be accountable in other circumstances because of the Light of Christ they possess (see 2 Nephi 9:25; Moroni 7:16–19). The Savior, who is our judge and who has assured a righteous judgment, will distinguish these circumstances (see Mormon 3:20; Moses 6:53–57). And He has paid the price for both—the former unconditionally and the latter upon the condition of repentance.

27. Alma 36:21.
28. See Mosiah 3:11; see also D. Todd Christofferson, "Redemption," *Ensign* or *Liahona,* May 2013, 110; Alma 7:11–12 ("He will take upon him the pains and the sicknesses of his people. . . . And he will take upon them their infirmities"); Isaiah 53:3–5 ("Surely he hath borne our griefs, and carried our sorrows"); 61:1–3 ("The Lord hath anointed me to . . . bind up the brokenhearted, . . . to appoint unto them that mourn in Zion, to give unto them beauty for ashes, the oil of joy for mourning"). It is instructive that the Savior quoted from these verses in Isaiah when He announced His Messiahship: "This day is this scripture fulfilled in your ears" (see Luke 4:16–21).
29. In the spirit world, "the gospel is preached to the ignorant, the unrepentant, and the rebellious so they can be freed from their bondage and go forward to the blessings a loving Heavenly Father has in store for them" (Dallin H. Oaks, "Trust in the Lord," *Ensign* or *Liahona,* Nov. 2019, 27). See 1 Peter 4:6; 2 Nephi 2:11–16; Doctrine and Covenants 128:19; 137:7–9; 138:31–35.
30. See Moses 6:54. President M. Russell Ballard taught this doctrine with respect to suicide: "Only the Lord knows all the details, and he it is who will judge our actions here on earth. When he does judge us, I feel he will take all things into consideration: our genetic and chemical makeup, our mental state, our intellectual capacity, the teachings we have received, the traditions of our fathers, our health, and so forth. We learn in the scriptures that the blood of Christ will atone for the sins of men 'who have died not knowing the will of God concerning them, or who have ignorantly sinned' (Mosiah 3:11)" ("Suicide: Some Things We Know, and Some We Do Not," *Ensign,* Oct. 1987, 8; *Tambuli,* Mar. 1988, 18).
31. See Jacob 6:5; Mosiah 29:20; 3 Nephi 9:14; Doctrine and Covenants 29:1.
32. See Helaman 8:15.
33. See Leviticus 6:4–5; Ezekiel 33:15–16; Helaman 5:17; Doctrine and Covenants 58:42–43.
34. It was just this sort of effort in which Alma himself engaged (see Alma 36:24).
35. President Boyd K. Packer taught this precept powerfully:

    "There are times you cannot mend that which you have broken. Perhaps the offense was long ago, or the injured refused your penance. Perhaps the damage was so severe that you cannot fix it no matter how desperately you want to.

    "Your repentance cannot be accepted unless there is a restitution. If you cannot undo what you have done, you are trapped. It is easy to understand how helpless and hopeless you then feel and why you might want to give up, just as Alma did. . . .

    "How all can be repaired, we do not know. It may not all be accomplished in this life. We know from visions and visitations that the servants of the Lord continue the work of redemption beyond the veil.

    "This knowledge should be as comforting to the innocent as it is to the guilty. I am thinking of parents who suffer unbearably for the mistakes of their wayward children and are losing hope" ("The Brilliant Morning of Forgiveness," 19–20).
36. See 3 Nephi 12:19; see also Matthew 6:12; 3 Nephi 13:11.
37. See John 15:12–13; 1 John 4:18; Dieter F. Uchtdorf, "Perfect Love Casteth Out Fear," *Ensign* or *Liahona,* May 2017, 107.

AN ESPECIALLY NOBLE CALLING
JOY D. JONES
Primary General President

I'm grateful to focus my remarks today on women's continuing roles in the Restoration. It is clear that throughout history women have held a distinctive place in our Heavenly Father's plan. President Russell M. Nelson taught, "It would be impossible to measure the influence that . . . women have, not only on families but also on the Lord's Church, as wives, mothers, and grandmothers; as sisters and aunts; as teachers and leaders; and especially as exemplars and devout defenders of the faith."[1]

In the early Relief Society in Nauvoo, 178 years ago, the Prophet Joseph Smith counseled the sisters to "live up to [their] privilege."[2] Their example teaches us today. They unitedly followed a prophet's voice and lived with steadfast faith in Jesus Christ as they helped lay the foundation we now stand upon. Sisters, it is our turn. We have a divine errand from the Lord, and our faithful, unique contributions are vital.

President Spencer W. Kimball explained: "To be a righteous woman during the winding up scenes on this earth, before the second coming of our Savior, is an especially noble calling. The righteous woman's strength and influence today can be tenfold what it might be in more tranquil times."[3]

President Nelson has likewise implored: "I plead with my sisters of [the] Church . . . to step forward! Take your rightful and needful place in your home, in your community, and in the kingdom of God—more than you ever have before."[4]

Recently, I was privileged, along with a group of Primary children, to meet with President Russell M. Nelson in the replica of the Smith family home in Palmyra, New York. Listen as our beloved prophet teaches the children what *they* can do to step forward.

SISTER JONES: "I'm curious to know if you might have a question that you would like to ask President Nelson. You're sitting here with the prophet. Is there anything that you've always wanted to ask a prophet? Yes, Pearl."

Pearl: "Is it hard to be a prophet? Are you, like, really busy?"

President Nelson: "Of course it's hard. Everything to do with becoming more like the Savior is difficult. For example, when God wanted to give the Ten Commandments to Moses, where did He tell Moses to go? Up on top of a mountain, on the top of Mount Sinai. So Moses had to walk all the way up to the top of that mountain to get the Ten Commandments. Now, Heavenly Father could have said, 'Moses, you start there, and I'll start here, and I'll meet you halfway.' No, the Lord loves effort, because effort brings rewards that can't come without it. For example, did you ever take piano lessons?"

Children: "Yes."

Pearl: "I take violin."

President Nelson: "And do you practice?"

Children: "Yes."

President Nelson: "What happens if you don't practice?"

Pearl: "You forget."

President Nelson: "Yes, you don't progress, do you? So the answer is yes, Pearl. It takes effort, a lot of hard work, a lot of study, and there's never an end. That's good! That's good, because we're always progressing. Even in the next life we're making progress."

President Nelson's response to these precious children extends to each one of us. The Lord loves effort, and effort brings rewards. We keep practicing. We are always progressing as long as we are striving to follow the Lord.[5] He doesn't expect perfection today. We keep climbing our personal Mount Sinai. As in times past, our journey does indeed take effort, hard work, and study, but our commitment to progress brings eternal rewards.[6]

What more do we learn from the Prophet Joseph Smith and the First Vision about effort, hard work, and study? The First Vision gives us direction in *our* unique, continuing roles. As women of faith, we can draw principles of truth from the Prophet Joseph's experiences that provide insights for receiving our own revelation. For example:

We labor under difficulties.

We turn to the scriptures to receive wisdom to act.

We demonstrate our faith and trust in God.

We exert our power to plead with God to help us thwart the adversary's influence.

We offer up the desires of our hearts to God.

We focus on His light guiding our life choices and resting upon us when we turn to Him.

We realize He knows each of us by name and has individual roles for us to fulfill.[7]

In addition, Joseph Smith restored the knowledge that we have divine potential and eternal worth. Because of that relationship with our Heavenly Father, I believe He *expects* us to receive revelation from Him.

The Lord instructed Emma Smith to "receive the Holy Ghost," learn much, "lay aside the things of this world, . . . seek for the things of a better," and "cleave unto [her] covenants" with God.[8] Learning is integral to progression, especially as the constant companionship of the Holy Ghost teaches us what is needful for each of us to lay aside—meaning that which could *distract* us or *delay* our progression.

President Nelson said, "I plead with you to increase your spiritual capacity to receive revelation."[9] Our prophet's words are continually with me as I contemplate women's ability to step forward. He pleads with us, which indicates priority. He is teaching us how to survive spiritually in a sin-sick world by receiving and acting on revelation.[10] As we do so, honoring and living the Lord's commandments, we are promised, even as Emma Smith was, "a crown of righteousness."[11] The Prophet Joseph taught of the importance of *knowing* that the path we are pursuing in this lifetime is approved of God. Without that knowledge, we "will grow weary in [our] minds, and faint."[12]

In this conference, we will hear truths that inspire us to change, improve, and purify our lives. Through personal revelation, we can prevent what some call "general conference overwhelm"—when we leave so determined to do it *all* now. Women wear many hats, but it is impossible, and unnecessary, to wear them all at once. The Spirit helps us determine which work to focus on today.[13]

The Lord's loving influence through the Holy Ghost helps us know *His* priority for our progression. Heeding personal revelation leads to *personal* progression.[14] We listen and act.[15] The Lord said, "Ask the Father in my name in faith, believing that you shall receive, and you shall have the Holy Ghost, which manifesteth all things which are expedient."[16] Our continuing role is to receive continuing revelation.

As we attain a greater degree of proficiency at doing so, we can receive more power in our individual roles to minister and accomplish the work of salvation and exaltation—to truly "lay aside the things of this world, and seek for the things of a better."[17] We can then more effectively inspire our rising generation to do the same.

Brothers and sisters, we all seek God's power in our lives.[18] There is beautiful unity between women and men in accomplishing God's work today. We access the power of the priesthood through covenants, made first in the waters of baptism and then within the walls of holy temples.[19] President Nelson taught us, "Every woman and every man who makes covenants with God and keeps those covenants, and who participates worthily in priesthood ordinances, has direct access to the power of God."[20]

My personal admission today is that as a woman I didn't realize, earlier in my life, that *I* had access, through my covenants, to the power of the priesthood.[21] Sisters, I pray that we will recognize and cherish priesthood power as we "cleave unto [our] covenants,"[22] embrace the truths of the scriptures, and heed the words of our living prophets.

Let us boldly declare our devotion to our Heavenly Father and our Savior, "with unshaken faith in him, relying wholly upon the merits of him who is mighty to save."[23] Let us joyfully continue this journey toward our highest spiritual potential and help those around us to do the same through love, service, leadership, and compassion.

Elder James E. Talmage tenderly reminded us, "The world's greatest champion of woman and womanhood is Jesus the Christ."[24] In the final analysis of women's continuing roles in the Restoration, and for us all, what role is preeminent? I testify that it is to *hear* Him,[25] to follow Him,[26] to trust Him,[27] and to become an extension of His love.[28] I know He lives.[29] In the sacred name of Jesus Christ, amen.

Notes

1. Russell M. Nelson, "A Plea to My Sisters," *Ensign* or *Liahona,* Nov. 2015, 95–96.
2. Joseph Smith, in "Nauvoo Relief Society Minute Book," 38, josephsmithpapers.org.
3. *Teachings of Presidents of the Church: Spencer W. Kimball* (2006), 217.
4. Russell M. Nelson, "A Plea to My Sisters," 97.
5. See Doctrine and Covenants 58:26–28.
6. See Doctrine and Covenants 6:33.
7. See Joseph Smith—History 1:11–17.
8. Doctrine and Covenants 25:8, 10, 13.
9. Russell M. Nelson, "Revelation for the Church, Revelation for Our Lives," *Ensign* or *Liahona,* May 2018, 96.
10. See 2 Nephi 9:39.
11. Doctrine and Covenants 25:15.
12. *Lectures on Faith* (1985), 68.
13. See Doctrine and Covenants 42:61.
14. President Henry B. Eyring said:

    "Now, if you and I were visiting alone (I wish we could be), where you felt free to ask whatever you wanted to ask, I can imagine your saying something like this: 'Oh, Brother Eyring, I've felt some of the things you have described. The Holy Ghost has touched my heart and mind from time to time. But I will need it consistently if I am not to be overcome or deceived. Is that possible? Is it possible, and, if it is, what will it take to receive that blessing?'

    "Well, let's start with the first part of your question. Yes, it is possible. Whenever I need that reassurance—and I need it from time to time too—I remember two brothers. Nephi and Lehi, and the other servants of the Lord laboring with them, faced fierce opposition. They were serving in an increasingly wicked world. They had to deal with terrible deceptions. So I take courage—and so can you—from the words in this one verse of Helaman. The reassurance is tucked into the account of all that happened in an entire year, almost as if to the writer it was not surprising. Listen:

    "'And in the seventy and ninth year there began to be much strife. But it came to pass that Nephi and Lehi, and many of their brethren who knew concerning the true points of doctrine, having many revelations daily, therefore they did preach unto the people, insomuch that they did put an end to their strife in that same year.' [Helaman 11:23]

    "They had 'many revelations daily.' So, for you and for me, that answers your first question. Yes, it is possible to have the companionship of the Holy Ghost sufficiently to have many revelations daily. It will not be easy. But it is possible. What it will require will be different for each person because we start from where we are in our unique set of experiences in life" ("Gifts of the Spirit for Hard Times" [Brigham Young University fireside, Sept. 10, 2006], 3–4, speeches.byu.edu).
15. See 2 Nephi 2:16.
16. Doctrine and Covenants 18:18.
17. Doctrine and Covenants 25:10.
18. See Doctrine and Covenants 121:26, 33, 41, 45–46.
19. See Doctrine and Covenants 84:19–21.

20. Russell M. Nelson, "Spiritual Treasures," *Ensign* or *Liahona,* Nov. 2019, 77.
21. See Russell M. Nelson, "Spiritual Treasures," 76–79; Dallin H. Oaks, "The Keys and Authority of the Priesthood," *Ensign* or *Liahona,* May 2014, 49–52; Henry B. Eyring, "Women and Gospel Learning in the Home," *Ensign* or *Liahona,* Nov. 2018, 58–60.
22. Doctrine and Covenants 25:13.
23. 2 Nephi 31:19.
24. James E. Talmage, *Jesus the Christ,* 3rd ed. (1916), 475.
25. See Joseph Smith—History 1:17.
26. See Matthew 4:19–20.
27. See Proverbs 3:5–6; Doctrine and Covenants 11:12.
28. See John 13:34; Moroni 7:47.
29. See 2 Nephi 33:6; Doctrine and Covenants 76:22.

SPIRITUALLY DEFINING MEMORIES

ELDER NEIL L. ANDERSEN
Of the Quorum of the Twelve Apostles

Eighteen years after the First Vision, the Prophet Joseph Smith wrote an extensive account of his experience. He had faced opposition, persecution, harassment, threats, and brutal attacks.[1] Yet he continued to boldly testify of his First Vision: "I had actually seen a light, and in the midst of that light I saw two Personages, and they did in reality speak to me; and though I was hated and persecuted for saying that I had seen a vision, yet it was true. . . . I knew it, and I knew that God knew it, and I could not deny it."[2]

In his difficult hours, Joseph's memory reached back nearly two decades to the certainty of God's love for him and the events that welcomed in the long-foretold Restoration. Reflecting on his spiritual journey, Joseph said: "I don't blame any one for not believing my history. If I had not experienced what I have, I would not have believed it myself."[3]

But the experiences were real, and he never forgot or denied them, quietly confirming his testimony as he moved to Carthage. "I am going like a lamb to the slaughter," he said, "but I am calm as a summer's morning; I have a conscience void of offense towards God, and towards all men."[4]

Your Spiritually Defining Experiences

There is a lesson for us in the Prophet Joseph's example. Along with the peaceful direction we receive from the Holy Ghost, from time to time, God powerfully and very personally assures each of us that He knows us and loves us and that He is blessing us specifically and openly. Then, in our moments of difficulty, the Savior brings these experiences back into our mind.

Think of your own life. Over the years, I have listened to thousands of profoundly spiritual experiences from Latter-day Saints all across the world, confirming to me beyond any question that God knows and loves each of us and that He eagerly desires to reveal

Himself to us. These experiences may come at pivotal times in our lives or in what may at first seem as uneventful happenings, but they are always accompanied by an exceptionally strong spiritual confirmation of the love of God.

Remembering these spiritually defining experiences takes us to our knees, declaring as did the Prophet Joseph: "What I received was from heaven. I know it, and I know that God knows that I know it."[5]

Four Examples

Reflect on your own spiritually defining memories as I share a few examples from others.

Years ago, an elderly stake patriarch with two failing heart valves pleaded for then-Dr. Russell M. Nelson to intervene, although at that time there was not a surgical solution for the damaged second valve. Dr. Nelson finally agreed to do the surgery. Here are President Nelson's words:

"After relieving the obstruction of the first valve, we exposed the second valve. We found it to be intact but so badly dilated that it could no longer function as it should. While examining this valve, a message was distinctly impressed upon my mind: *Reduce the circumference of the ring*. I announced that message to my assistant. 'The valve tissue will be sufficient *if* we can effectively reduce the ring toward its normal size.'

"But how? . . . A picture came vividly to my mind, showing how stitches could be placed—to make a pleat here and a tuck there. . . . I still remember that mental image—complete with dotted lines where sutures should be placed. The repair was completed as diagrammed in my mind. We tested the valve and found the leak to be reduced remarkably. My assistant said, 'It's a miracle.'"[6] The patriarch lived for many years.

Dr. Nelson had been directed. And he knew that God knew that he knew he had been directed.

Kathy and I first met Beatrice Magré in France 30 years ago. Beatrice recently told me of an experience that impacted her spiritual life shortly after her baptism as a teenager. Here are her words:

"The youth of our branch had traveled with their leaders to Lacanau Beach, an hour and a half from Bordeaux.

"Before returning home, one of the leaders decided to take a last swim and dove into the waves with his glasses. When he resurfaced, his glasses had disappeared. . . . They were lost in the ocean.

"The loss of his glasses would prevent him from driving his car. We would be stranded far from home.

"A sister filled with faith suggested that we pray.

"I murmured that praying would avail us absolutely nothing, and I uneasily joined the group to pray publicly as we stood waist-deep in the murky water.

"Once the prayer was over, I stretched my arms to splash everyone. As I was sweeping the ocean's surface, his pair of glasses rested in my hand. A powerful feeling pierced my soul that God does actually hear and answer our prayers."[7]

Forty-five years later, she recalled it as if it had happened yesterday. Beatrice had been blessed, and she knew that God knew that she knew that she had been blessed.

The experiences of President Nelson and Sister Magré were very different, yet for both, an unforgettable spiritually defining memory of God's love was embedded in their hearts.

These defining events often come in learning about the restored gospel or in sharing the gospel with others.

In São Paulo, Brazil, in 2004, Floripes Luzia Damasio of the Ipatinga Brazil Stake was 114 years old. Speaking of her conversion, Sister Damasio told me that missionaries in her village had given a priesthood blessing to a critically ill baby who miraculously recovered. She wanted to know more. As she prayed about their message, an undeniable witness of the Spirit confirmed to her that Joseph Smith was a prophet of God. At 103, she was baptized, and at 104, she was endowed. Every year after, she made the 14-hour bus ride to spend a week in the temple. Sister Damasio had received a heavenly confirmation, and she knew that God knew that she knew that the witness was true.

Here is a spiritual memory from my first mission to France 48 years ago.

While tracting, my companion and I left a Book of Mormon with an elderly woman. When we returned to the woman's apartment about a week later, she opened the door. Before any words were spoken, I felt a tangible spiritual power. The intense feelings continued as Madame Alice Audubert invited us in and told us she had read the Book of Mormon and knew that it was true. As we left her apartment that day, I prayed, "Heavenly Father, please help me to never forget what I have just felt." I never have.

In a seemingly ordinary moment, at a door much like hundreds of other doors, I had felt the power of heaven. And I knew that God knew that I knew that a window of heaven had been opened.

Individualized and Undeniable

These spiritually defining moments come at different times and in different ways, individualized for each of us.

Think of your favorite examples in the scriptures. Those listening to the Apostle Peter "were pricked in their heart[s]."[8] The Lamanite woman Abish believed the "remarkable vision of her father."[9] And a voice came into the mind of Enos.[10]

My friend Clayton Christensen described an experience during a very prayerful reading of the Book of Mormon this way: "A beautiful, warm, loving Spirit . . . surrounded me and permeated my soul, enveloping me in a feeling of love that I had not imagined I could feel [and these feelings continued night after night]."[11]

There are times when spiritual feelings go down into our heart like fire, illuminating our soul. Joseph Smith explained that we sometimes receive "sudden strokes of ideas" and occasionally the pure flow of intelligence.[12]

President Dallin H. Oaks, in responding to a sincere man who claimed never to have had such an experience, counseled, "Perhaps your prayers have been answered again and again, but you have had your expectations fixed on a sign so grand or a voice so loud that you think you have had no answer."[13] The Savior Himself spoke of a people with great faith who "were [blessed] with fire and with the Holy Ghost, [but who] knew it not."[14]

How Do You Hear Him?

We have recently heard President Russell M. Nelson say: "I invite you to think deeply and often about this key question: How do *you* hear Him? I also invite you to take steps to hear Him better and more often."[15] He repeated that invitation this morning.

We hear Him in our prayers, in our homes, in the scriptures, in our hymns, as we worthily partake of the sacrament, as we declare our faith, as we serve others, and as we attend the temple with fellow believers. Spiritually defining moments come as we prayerfully listen to general conference and as we better keep the commandments. And children, these experiences are for you as well. Remember, Jesus "did teach and minister unto the children . . . and [the children] did speak . . . great and marvelous things."[16] The Lord said:

"[This knowledge is] given by my Spirit unto you, . . . and save it were by my power you could not have [it];

"Wherefore, you can testify that you have heard my voice, and know my words."[17]

We can "hear Him" because of the blessing of the Savior's incomparable Atonement.

While we cannot choose the timing of receiving these defining moments, President Henry B. Eyring gave this counsel in our preparation: "Tonight, and tomorrow night, you might pray and ponder, asking the questions: Did God send a message that was just for me? Did I see His hand in my life or the lives of my [family]?"[18] Faith, obedience, humility, and real intent open the windows of heaven.[19]

You might think of your spiritual memories this way. With constant prayer, a determination to keep our covenants, and the gift of the Holy Ghost, we navigate our way through life. When personal difficulty, doubt, or discouragement darken our path, or when world conditions beyond our control lead us to wonder about the future, the spiritually defining memories from our book of life are like luminous stones that help brighten the road ahead, assuring us that God knows us, loves us, and has sent His Son, Jesus Christ, to help us return home. And when someone sets their defining memories aside and is lost or confused, we turn them toward the Savior as we share our faith and memories with them, helping them rediscover those precious spiritual moments they once treasured.

Some experiences are so sacred that we guard them in our spiritual memory and do not share them.[20]

"Angels speak by the power of the Holy Ghost; wherefore, they speak the words of Christ."[21]

"Angels [have not] ceased to minister unto the children of men.

"For behold, they are subject unto [Christ], to minister according to . . . his command, showing themselves unto them of strong faith and a firm mind in every form of godliness."[22]

And "the Comforter, which is the Holy Ghost, . . . shall teach you all things, and bring all things to your remembrance."[23]

Embrace your sacred memories. Believe them. Write them down. Share them with your family. Trust that they come to you from your Heavenly Father and His Beloved Son.[24] Let them bring patience to your doubts and understanding to your difficulties.[25] I promise you that as you willingly acknowledge and carefully treasure the spiritually defining events in your life, more and more will come to you. Heavenly Father knows you and loves you!

Jesus is the Christ, His gospel has been restored, and as we remain faithful, I witness we will be His forever, in the name of Jesus Christ, amen.

Notes

1. See *Saints: The Story of the Church of Jesus Christ in the Latter Days*, vol. 1, *The Standard of Truth, 1815–1846* (2018), 150–53; see also Joseph Smith, "History, 1838–1856, volume A-1 [23 December 1805–30 August 1834]," 205–9, josephsmithpapers.org; Saints, 1:365–66.
2. Joseph Smith—History 1:25.
3. *Teachings of Presidents of the Church: Joseph Smith* (2007), 525.
4. Doctrine and Covenants 135:4.
5. I have always been impressed with the words in Joseph Smith—History: "I had seen a vision; I knew it, and I knew that God knew it" (Joseph Smith—History 1:25). He would have to stand before God and acknowledge that these events in the Sacred Grove actually happened in his life and that his life could never be the same because of it. About 25 years ago, I first heard a variation of this phrase by Elder Neal A. Maxwell. He gave this example: "Long ago in May 1945 there was such a moment for me on the island of Okinawa at age eighteen. There was

certainly no heroism on my part but rather a blessing for me and others during the shelling of our position by Japanese artillery. After repeated shellings which overshot our position, the enemy artillery finally zeroed in. They should have then fired for effect, but there was a divine response to at least one frightened, selfish prayer. The shelling halted. . . . I had been blessed, and I knew that God knew that I knew" ("Becoming a Disciple," *Ensign,* June 1996, 19).

Elder Maxwell added not only that he knew, and not only that God knew, but that God knew that he knew he had been blessed. Symbolically for me this raises the accountability a step higher. At times, our Heavenly Father accompanies a blessing given to us with an intense spiritual confirmation that the heavens intervened on our behalf. There is no denying it. It stays with us, and if we are honest and faithful, it will shape our life in the coming years. "I had been blessed, and I knew that God knew that I knew that I had been blessed."

6. Russell M. Nelson, "Sweet Power of Prayer," *Ensign* or *Liahona,* May 2003, 8.
7. Personal story from Beatrice Magré shared with Elder Andersen on Oct. 29, 2019; follow-up email on Jan. 24, 2020.
8. Acts 2:37.
9. Alma 19:16.
10. See Enos 1:5.
11. Clayton M. Christensen, "The Most Useful Piece of Knowledge," *New Era,* Jan. 2009, 41; *Liahona,* Jan. 2009, 23.
12. See *Teachings: Joseph Smith,* 132.
13. Dallin H. Oaks, *Life's Lessons Learned: Personal Reflections* (2011), 116.
14. 3 Nephi 9:20.
15. Russell M. Nelson, "'How Do You #HearHim?' A Special Invitation," Feb. 26, 2020, blog .ChurchofJesusChrist.org.
16. 3 Nephi 26:14.
17. Doctrine and Covenants 18:35–36. Feelings always accompany spiritual knowledge. "Ye are swift to do iniquity but slow to remember the Lord your God. Ye have seen an angel, and he spake unto you; yea, ye have heard his voice from time to time; and he hath spoken unto you in a still small voice, but ye were past feeling, that ye could not feel his words" (1 Nephi 17:45).
18. Henry B. Eyring, "O Remember, Remember," *Ensign* or *Liahona,* Nov. 2007, 69.
19. See 2 Nephi 31:13; Moroni 10:4. President Dallin H. Oaks visited our mission in Bordeaux, France, in 1991. He explained to our missionaries that real intent means that the person praying is saying to the Lord something like this: "I do not ask out of curiosity but with total sincerity to act on the answer to my prayer. If Thou wilt give me this answer, I will act to change my life. I will respond."
20. "It is given unto many to know the mysteries of God; nevertheless they are laid under a strict command that they shall not impart only according to the portion of his word which he doth grant unto the children of men, according to the heed and diligence which they give unto him" (Alma 12:9).

    Elder Neal A. Maxwell said: "It takes inspiration to know when to share [spiritual experiences]. I recall hearing President Marion G. Romney, who combined wit and wisdom, say, 'We'd have more spiritual experiences if we didn't talk so much about them'" ("Called to Serve" [Brigham Young University devotional, Mar. 27, 1994], 9, speeches.byu.edu).
21. 2 Nephi 32:3.
22. Moroni 7:29–30.
23. John 14:26.
24. The truths of the gospel are available to all. In the week prior to conference, after my talk was completed, I was spiritually drawn to a book called *Divine Signatures: The Confirming Hand of God* (2010), authored by Gerald N. Lund, who served as a General Authority Seventy from 2002 to 2008. To my delight, Brother Lund's words were a beautiful second witness to the principles shared in this conference talk and will be enjoyed by anyone desiring to study more about spiritually defining memories.
25. One of President Thomas S. Monson's favorite quotes is from the Scottish poet James M. Barrie: "God gave us memories, that we might have June roses in the December of our lives" (in Thomas S. Monson, "Think to Thank," *Ensign,* Nov. 1998, 19; *Liahona,* Jan. 1999, 22). The same is true with spiritual memories. They may be most helpful in the cold, trying times of our lives when we need those "June" spiritual memories.

DEEP IN OUR HEART

DOUGLAS D. HOLMES
Recently Released First Counselor in the Young Men General Presidency

Sisters and brothers, what a wonderful time we live in. As we celebrate the beginning of the Restoration, it is also appropriate to celebrate the ongoing Restoration that we are witnessing. I rejoice with you to live in this day.[1] The Lord continues to put in place, through His prophets, all that is needed to help us prepare to receive Him.[2]

One of those needed things is the new Children and Youth initiative. Many of you are familiar with this program's emphasis on setting goals, new emblems of belonging, and For the Strength of Youth conferences. But we must not let those cloud our view of the principles the program is built on and their purpose: to help get the gospel of Jesus Christ deep in the hearts of our children and youth.[3]

I believe as we come to see these principles more clearly, we will recognize this as more than a program for members ages 8 to 18. We will see how the Lord is trying to help us—all of us—get His gospel deeper in our hearts. I pray the Holy Ghost will help us learn together.

Relationships—"Be with Them"[4]

The first principle is relationships. Because they are such a natural part of the Church of Jesus Christ, we sometimes forget the importance of relationships in our ongoing journey to Christ. We are not expected to find or walk the covenant path alone. We need love and support from parents, other family members, friends, and leaders who are also walking the path.

These kinds of relationships take time. Time to be together. Time to laugh, play, learn, and serve together. Time to appreciate each other's interests and challenges. Time to be open and honest with each other as we strive to be better together. These relationships are one of the primary purposes of gathering as families, quorums, classes, and congregations. They are the foundation for effective ministering.[5]

Elder Dale G. Renlund gave us a key to developing these relationships when he said: "To effectively serve others we must see them . . . through Heavenly Father's eyes. Only then can we begin to comprehend the true worth of a soul. Only then can we sense the love that Heavenly Father has for all His children."[6]

Seeing others as God does is a gift. I invite all of us to seek for this gift. As our eyes are opened to see,[7] we will also be able to help others see themselves as God does.[8] President Henry B. Eyring emphasized the power of this when he said: "What will matter most is what [others] learn from [you] about who they really are and what they can really become. My guess is that they won't learn it so much from lectures. They will get it from *feelings* of who you are, who you think they are, and what you think they might become."[9] Helping others understand their true identity and purpose is one of the greatest gifts we can give.[10] Seeing others and ourselves as God does knits our hearts "together in unity and in love."[11]

With ever-increasing secular forces pulling at us, we need the strength that comes from loving relationships. So as we plan activities, meetings, and other gatherings, let us remember an overarching purpose of these gatherings is to build loving relationships that unite us and help get the gospel of Jesus Christ deeper in our hearts.[12]

Revelation, Agency, and Repentance—
"Connect Them with Heaven"[13]

Of course, it's not enough just to be bound together. There are many groups and organizations that achieve unity around a variety of causes. But the unity we seek is to be one in Christ, to connect ourselves with Him.[14] To connect our hearts with heaven, we need individual spiritual experiences, as Elder Andersen just eloquently spoke to us about.[15] Those experiences come as the Holy Ghost carries the word and love of God to our mind and heart.[16]

This revelation comes through the scriptures, especially the Book of Mormon; through inspired words of living prophets and other faithful disciples; and through the still, small voice.[17] These words are more than ink on a page, sound waves in our ears, thoughts in our minds, or feelings in our hearts. The word of God is spiritual power.[18] It is truth and light.[19] It is how we hear Him! The word initiates and increases our faith in Christ and fuels within us a desire to become more like the Savior—that is, to repent and walk the covenant path.[20]

Last April, President Russell M. Nelson helped us understand the central role of repentance in this revelatory journey.[21] He said: "When we choose to repent, we choose to change! We allow the Savior to transform us into the best version of ourselves. . . . We choose to become more like Jesus Christ!"[22] This process of change, fueled by the word of God, is how we connect with heaven.

Underlying President Nelson's invitation to repent is the principle of agency. We must *choose* repentance for ourselves. The gospel can't be forced into our hearts. As Elder Renlund said, "Our Heavenly Father's goal in parenting is not to have His children *do* what is right; it is to have His children *choose* to do what is right."[23]

In the programs replaced by Children and Youth, there were over 500 different requirements to complete in order to receive various recognitions.[24] Today, there is essentially one. It is an invitation to *choose* to become more like the Savior. We do this by receiving the word of God through the Holy Ghost and allowing Christ to change us into the best version of ourselves.

This is far more than an exercise in goal setting or self-improvement. Goals are simply a tool that helps us connect with heaven through revelation, agency, and repentance—to come unto Christ and receive His gospel deeper in our hearts.

Engagement and Sacrifice—"Let Them Lead"[25]

Finally, to get the gospel of Jesus Christ deep in our hearts, we need to engage in it—to give our time and talents to it, to sacrifice for it.[26] We all want to live a life of meaning, and this is especially true of the rising generation. They desire a cause.

The gospel of Jesus Christ is the greatest cause in the world.

President Ezra Taft Benson said: "We are commanded by God to take this gospel to all the world. That is the cause that must unite us today. Only the gospel will save the world from the calamity of its own self-destruction. Only the gospel will unite men [and women] of all races and nationalities in peace. Only the gospel will bring joy, happiness, and salvation to the human family."[27]

Elder David A. Bednar promised, "As we empower the youth by inviting and allowing them to act, the Church will move forward in miraculous ways."[28] Too often we have not invited and allowed the youth to sacrifice for this great cause of Christ. Elder Neal A. Maxwell observed, "If [our] youth are too underwhelmed [by God's work], they are more likely to be overwhelmed by the world."[29]

The Children and Youth program focuses on empowering the youth. They choose their own goals. Quorum and class presidencies are placed in their proper role. The ward youth council, just like the ward council, focuses on the work of salvation and exaltation.[30] And quorums and classes begin their meetings by counseling about how to do the work God has given them.[31]

President Nelson said to the youth of the Church: "If you choose to, if you want to, . . . you can be a big part of something big, something grand, something majestic! . . . You are among the best the Lord has *ever* sent to this world. You have the capacity to be smarter and wiser and have more impact on the world than any previous generation!"[32] On another occasion, President Nelson told the youth: "I have complete confidence in you. I love you, and so does the Lord. We're His people, engaged together in His holy work."[33] Young people, can you feel the trust President Nelson has in you and how important you are to this work?

Parents and adult leaders, I invite you to see the youth as President Nelson does. As the youth feel your love and trust, as you encourage and teach them how to lead—and then get out of their way—they will amaze you with their insights, abilities, and commitment to the gospel.[34] They will feel the joy of choosing to engage in and sacrifice for the cause of Christ. His gospel will get deeper into their hearts, and the work will move forward in miraculous ways.

Promise and Testimony

I promise, as we focus on these principles—relationships, revelation, agency, repentance, and sacrifice—the gospel of Jesus Christ will sink deeper in all our hearts. We will see the Restoration move forward to its ultimate purpose, the redemption of Israel and the establishment of Zion,[35] where Christ will reign as King of kings.

I testify that God continues to do all things necessary to prepare His people for that day. May we see His hand in this glorious work as we all strive to "come unto Christ, and be perfected in him."[36] In the name of Jesus Christ, amen.

Notes

1. See Doctrine and Covenants 45:12. President Nelson said: "Just think of the excitement and urgency of it all: every prophet commencing with Adam has seen our day. And every prophet has talked about *our* day, when Israel would be gathered and the world would be prepared for the Second Coming of the Savior. Think of it! Of all the people who have ever lived on planet earth, *we* are the ones who get to participate in this final, great gathering event. How exciting is that!" ("Hope of Israel" [worldwide youth devotional, June 3, 2018], HopeofIsrael.ChurchofJesusChrist.org).

    Elder Jeffrey R. Holland taught:

    "What a terrific time to be alive!

    "The gospel of Jesus Christ is the most certain, the most secure, the most reliable, and the most rewarding truth on earth and in heaven, in time and in eternity. Nothing—not anything, not anyone, not any influence—will keep this Church from fulfilling its mission and realizing its destiny declared from before the foundation of the world. . . . There is no need to be afraid or tentative about the future.

    "Unlike every other era before us, this dispensation will not experience an institutional apostasy; it will not see a loss of priesthood keys; it will not suffer a cessation of revelation from the voice of Almighty God. . . . What a day in which to live!

    " . . . If you haven't noticed, I am bullish about the latter days. . . . Believe. Rise up. Be faithful. And make the most of the remarkable day in which we live!" (Facebook post, May 27, 2015; see also "Be Not Afraid, Only Believe" [address to Church Educational System religious educators, Feb. 6, 2015], broadcasts.ChurchofJesusChrist.org).
2. See John 1:12.
3. Shortly after we were called as the Young Men General Presidency, President Henry B. Eyring discussed with us the unique challenges and opportunities the youth of the Church face today. He counseled us to focus on those things that would help get the gospel of Jesus Christ down deep in their hearts. That counsel has been a beacon for us as the Young Men Presidency.
4. See "Be with Them," ChurchofJesusChrist.org/callings/aaronic-priesthood-quorums/my-calling/leader-instruction/be-with-them.
5. See Mosiah 18:25; Moroni 6:5.
6. Dale G. Renlund, "Through God's Eyes," *Ensign* or *Liahona,* Nov. 2015, 94; see also Moses 1:4–6.

    President Thomas S. Monson taught: "We have the responsibility to see individuals not as they are but rather as they can become. I would plead with you to think of them in this way" ("See Others as They May Become," *Ensign* or *Liahona,* Nov. 2012, 70).

    Elder Neal A. Maxwell taught: "Too often, a young person's outward *non-compliance* with Church standards, or his seemingly confrontive questions, or his expressed doubts get him quickly labeled. The results can be distance and, sometimes, disaffiliation. True love does not like labels!" ("Unto the Rising Generation," *Ensign,* Apr. 1985, 9).

7. See 2 Kings 6:17.
8. Stephen L. Richards, as a member of the First Presidency, said, "The highest type of discernment is that which perceives in others and uncovers for them their better natures, the good inherent within them" (in Conference Report, Apr. 1950, 162; in David A. Bednar, "Quick to Observe," *Ensign,* Dec. 2006, 35; *Liahona,* Dec. 2006, 19). See also 2 Kings 6:17.
9. Henry B. Eyring, "Teaching Is a Moral Act" (address at Brigham Young University, Aug. 27, 1991), 3, speeches.byu.edu; emphasis added; see also Henry B. Eyring, "Help Them Aim High," *Ensign* or *Liahona,* Nov. 2012, 60–67.
10. See Moses 1:3–6.
11. Mosiah 18:21; see also Moses 7:18.
12. "Young men who have strong, positive relationships with an active [Latter-day Saint] family, peers, and leaders, which help them develop a relationship with their Heavenly Father, are most likely to stay active. Specific program elements—such as the Sunday curriculum, [Young Men] activity program, personal achievement expectations . . . may have little effect independent of those relationships. . . . The important question is not how completely specific program elements are implemented but how they contribute to positive relationships that strengthen the religious identity of [Latter-day Saint] young men" ("Be with Them," ChurchofJesusChrist.org/callings/aaronic-priesthood-quorums/my-calling/leader-instruction/be-with-them).
13. See "Connect Them with Heaven," ChurchofJesusChrist.org/callings/aaronic-priesthood-quorums/my-calling/leader-instruction/connect-them-with-heaven.
14. See John 15:1–5; 17:11; Philippians 4:13; 1 John 2:6; Jacob 1:7; Omni 1:26; Moroni 10:32.
15. The scriptures are full of examples of this; here are just two: 1 Nephi 2:16; Enos 1:1–4.
16. See Luke 24:32; 2 Nephi 33:1–2; Jacob 3:2; Moroni 8:26; Doctrine and Covenants 8:2–3.
17. See 2 Timothy 3:15–16; Doctrine and Covenants 68:3–4; 88:66; 113:10.
18. See 1 Thessalonians 1:5; Alma 26:13; 31:5; Helaman 3:29; 5:17; Doctrine and Covenants 21:4–6; 42:61; 43:8–10; 50:17–22; 68:4.
19. See John 6:63; 17:17; Alma 5:7; Doctrine and Covenants 84:43–45; 88:66; 93:36.
20. See John 15:3; 1 Peter 1:23; Mosiah 1:5; Alma 5:7, 11–13; 32:28, 41–42; 36:26; 62:45; Helaman 14:13.
21. See 2 Nephi 31:19–21; 32:3, 5.
22. Russell M. Nelson, "We Can Do Better and Be Better," *Ensign* or *Liahona,* May 2019, 67.
23. Dale G. Renlund, "Choose You This Day," *Ensign* or *Liahona,* Nov. 2018, 104.
24. This figure includes requirements of the Scouting programs, which until recently were part of the Church's activity program for boys and young men, primarily in the United States and Canada. In areas that did not participate in Scouting, the number of requirements was over 200. In addition, the various activity programs for boys, girls, young men, and young women were structured differently, making the whole experience more complex for families.
25. See "Let Them Lead," ChurchofJesusChrist.org/callings/aaronic-priesthood-quorums/my-calling/leader-instruction/let-them-lead.
26. See Omni 1:26; 3 Nephi 9:20; 12:19; Doctrine and Covenants 64:34. "A religion that does not require the sacrifice of all things never has power sufficient to produce the faith necessary unto life and salvation" (*Lectures on Faith* [1985], 69).
27. Ezra Taft Benson, *The Teachings of Ezra Taft Benson* (1988), 167; in *Preach My Gospel: A Guide to Missionary Service* (2019), 13; see also Russell M. Nelson, "Hope of Israel," HopeofIsrael.ChurchofJesusChrist.org.
28. Meeting with Elder David A. Bednar; see also "2020 Temple and Family History Leadership Instruction," Feb. 27, 2020, ChurchofJesusChrist.org/family-history.
29. Neal A. Maxwell, "Unto the Rising Generation," 11. Elder Maxwell continued: "Functionally, how many deacons and teachers quorum presidencies consist of merely calling on someone to offer a prayer or pass the sacrament? Brethren, these really are special spirits, and they can do things of significance if given a chance!"
30. See *General Handbook: Serving in The Church of Jesus Christ of Latter-day Saints,* 2.2, ChurchofJesusChrist.org.
31. Several resources are available in the Gospel Library to help the youth lead, including "Quorum and Class Presidency Resources," "Using *Come, Follow Me—For Aaronic Priesthood Quorums and Young Women Classes,*" and in the resources for Young Women classes and Aaronic Priesthood quorums in "Ward or Branch Callings."

SATURDAY MORNING SESSION

32. Russell M. Nelson, "Hope of Israel," HopeofIsrael.ChurchofJesusChrist.org. During this same devotional, President Nelson said: "Our Heavenly Father has reserved many of His most noble spirits—perhaps, I might say, His finest team—for this final phase. Those noble spirits—those finest players, those heroes—are you!"
33. Russell M. Nelson, opening remarks in "Children and Youth: A Face to Face Event with Elder Gerrit W. Gong," Nov. 17, 2019, broadcasts.ChurchofJesusChrist.org.
34. President Nelson said: "We need to let the young people lead, particularly those who have been called and set apart to serve in class and quorum presidencies. Priesthood authority will have been delegated to them. They will learn how to receive inspiration in leading their class or quorum" (in "Children and Youth Introductory Video Presentation," Sept. 29, 2019, ChurchofJesusChrist.org).

Elder Quentin L. Cook said, "Our youth are being asked to take more individual responsibility at younger ages—without parents and leaders taking over what youth can do for themselves" ("Adjustments to Strengthen Youth," *Ensign* or *Liahona,* Nov. 2019, 40).

35. President George Q. Cannon taught: "God has reserved spirits for this dispensation who have the courage and determination to face the world, and all the powers of the evil one, visible and invisible, to proclaim the gospel and maintain the truth and establish and build up the Zion of our God fearless of all consequences. He has sent these spirits in this generation to lay the foundation of Zion never more to be overthrown, and to raise up a seed that will be righteous, and that will honor God, and honor Him supremely, and be obedient to Him under all circumstances" ("Remarks," *Deseret News,* May 31, 1866, 203); see also *Teachings of Presidents of the Church: Joseph Smith* (2007), 186.
36. Moroni 10:32.

PRAYERS OF FAITH

PRESIDENT HENRY B. EYRING
Second Counselor in the First Presidency

The prayer of Elder Maynes at the beginning of this first session of general conference is being answered. Inspiration has come to us through wonderful messages and beautiful music. The promise of President Russell M. Nelson that this conference will be memorable is already beginning to be fulfilled.

President Nelson has designated this year as "a bicentennial period commemorating 200 years since God the Father and His Beloved Son, Jesus Christ, appeared to Joseph Smith in a vision." President Nelson invited us to make a personal plan to prepare ourselves for this historic conference, which commemoration he said would be "a hinge point in the history of the Church, and your part is vital."[1]

Like me, perhaps you heard his message and asked yourself, "In what way is my part vital?" Perhaps you read and prayed about the events of the Restoration. Perhaps, more than ever before, you read the accounts of those few times when God the Father introduced His Beloved Son. Perhaps you read of the instances when the Savior spoke to the children of our Heavenly Father. I know I did all of those things and more.

I found references in my reading to the priesthood of God and the opening of dispensations. I was humbled as I realized that my preparation for this conference was a hinge point in my personal history. I felt changes in my heart. I felt new gratitude. I felt filled with joy at the prospect of being invited to participate in this celebration of the ongoing Restoration.

I imagine that others are feeling, because of careful preparation, more joyful, more optimistic, and more determined to serve in any capacity needed by the Lord.

The transcendent events we honor were the beginning of the prophesied last dispensation, in which the Lord is preparing His Church and His people, those who bear His name, to receive Him.

As part of our preparation for His coming, He will lift each of us so we may rise to spiritual challenges and opportunities unlike any seen in the history of this world.

In September 1840, the Prophet Joseph Smith and his counselors in the First Presidency declared the following: "The work of the Lord in these last days, is one of vast magnitude and almost beyond the comprehension of mortals. Its glories are past description, and its grandeur unsurpassable. It is the theme which has animated the bosom of prophets and righteous men from the creation of the world down through every succeeding generation to the present time; and it is truly the dispensation of the fullness of times, when all things which are in Christ Jesus, whether in heaven or on the earth, shall be gathered together in Him, and when all things shall be restored, as spoken of by all the holy prophets since the world began; for in it will take place the glorious fulfilment of the promises made to the fathers, while the manifestations of the power of the Most High will be great, glorious, and sublime."

They went on to say: "We feel disposed to go forward and unite our energies for the upbuilding of the Kingdom, and establishing the Priesthood in their fullness and glory. The work which has to be accomplished in the last days is one of vast importance, and will call into action the energy, skill, talent, and ability of the Saints, so that it may roll forth with that glory and majesty described by the prophet [Daniel] [see Daniel 2:34–35, 44–45]; and will consequently require the concentration of the Saints, to accomplish works of such magnitude and grandeur."[2]

Many of the specifics of what we will do and when we will do it in the unfolding Restoration are not yet revealed. Yet the First Presidency even in those early days knew some of the breadth and depth of the work the Lord has set before us. Here are a few examples of what we do know will take place:

Through His Saints, the Lord will offer the gift of His gospel "to every nation, kindred, tongue, and people."[3] Technology and miracles will continue to play a part—as will individual "fishers of men"[4] who minister with power and increasing faith.

We as a people will become more united amid increasing conflict. We will be gathered in the spiritual strength of groups and families filled with gospel light.

Even an unbelieving world will recognize The Church of Jesus Christ of Latter-day Saints and realize the power of God upon it. Faithful and brave disciples will fearlessly, humbly, and openly take upon them the name of Christ in their everyday lives.

How, then, can each of us participate in this work of such magnitude and grandeur? President Nelson has taught us how to grow in spiritual power. When we take repentance as a joyful opportunity because of our growing faith that Jesus is the Christ, when we understand and believe that Heavenly Father hears our every prayer, when we strive to obey and live the commandments, we grow in our power to receive continuing revelation. The Holy Ghost can be our constant companion. A feeling of light will stay with us even as the world around us becomes darker.

Joseph Smith is an example of how to grow in such spiritual power. He showed us that the prayer of faith is the key to revelation from God. He prayed in faith, believing that God the Father would answer his prayer. He prayed in faith, believing that only through Jesus Christ could he be freed from the guilt he felt for his sins. And he prayed in faith, believing that he needed to find the true Church of Jesus Christ to gain that forgiveness.

Throughout his prophetic ministry, Joseph Smith used prayers of faith to obtain continuous revelation. As we face today's challenges and those yet to come, we too will need to practice the same pattern. President Brigham Young said, "I do not know any other way for the Latter-day Saints than for every breath to be virtually a prayer for God to guide and direct his people."[5]

These words from the sacrament prayer should then describe our daily life: "Always remember him." "Him" refers to Jesus Christ. The next words, "and keep his commandments," suggest what it means for us to remember Him.[6] As we remember Jesus Christ always, we might ask in silent prayer, "What would He have me do?"

Such prayer, offered in faith in Jesus Christ, ushered in this last dispensation. And it will be at the heart of the part each of us will play in its continuing unfolding. I have found, as you have, wonderful examples of such prayer.

First is Joseph Smith. He asked in childlike faith what the Lord would have him do. His answer changed the history of the world.

To me, an important lesson comes from Joseph's response to Satan's assault as Joseph knelt to pray.

I know from experience that Satan and his servants try to make us feel that we must not pray. When Joseph Smith exerted all his powers to call upon God to deliver him from the power that tried to bind him, his prayer for relief was answered and Heavenly Father and Jesus Christ appeared.

Satan's attempt to thwart the beginning of the Restoration was so severe because Joseph's prayer was so important. You and I will have smaller parts to play in the ongoing Restoration. Yet the enemy of the Restoration will try to stop us from praying. The example of Joseph's faith and his determination can strengthen us in our resolve. This is one of many reasons why my prayers include thanks to Heavenly Father for the Prophet Joseph.

Enos in the Book of Mormon is another model for my prayer of faith as I try to play my part in the continuing Restoration. Whatever your part will be, you could take him as a personal mentor.

Like Joseph, Enos prayed in faith. He described his experience this way:

"And my soul hungered; and I kneeled down before my Maker, and I cried unto him in mighty prayer and supplication for mine own soul; and all the day long did I cry unto him; yea, and when the night came I did still raise my voice high that it reached the heavens.

"And there came a voice unto me, saying: Enos, thy sins are forgiven thee, and thou shalt be blessed.

"And I, Enos, knew that God could not lie; wherefore, my guilt was swept away.

"And I said: Lord, how is it done?

"And he said unto me: Because of thy faith in Christ, whom thou hast never before heard nor seen. And many years pass away before he shall manifest himself in the flesh; wherefore, go to, thy faith hath made thee whole."[7]

The lesson that has blessed me is in these words: "Because of thy faith in Christ, whom thou hast never before heard nor seen."

Joseph had faith in Christ to go into the grove and also to pray for release from the powers of Satan. He had not yet seen the Father and the Son, but he prayed in faith with all the energy of his heart.

The experience of Enos has taught me the same precious lesson. When I pray with faith, I have the Savior as my advocate with the Father and I can feel that my prayer reaches heaven. Answers come. Blessings are received. There is peace and joy even in hard times.

I remember when, as the newest member of the Quorum of the Twelve Apostles, I knelt in prayer with Elder David B. Haight. He was about the age I am now, with challenges I now experience myself. I remember his voice as he prayed. I didn't open my eyes to look, but it sounded to me as if he was smiling. He spoke with Heavenly Father with joy in his voice.

I can hear in my mind his happiness when he said, "In the name of Jesus Christ." It sounded to me as if Elder Haight felt the Savior was affirming at that moment the message he had prayed to the Father. And I was sure it would be received with a smile.

Our ability to make our vital contribution to the wonderful continuing Restoration will increase as we grow in our faith in Jesus Christ as our Savior and our Heavenly Father as our loving Father. As we pray in faith, we become a vital part in the Lord's work as He prepares the world for His Second Coming. I pray that we all may find joy in doing the work He invites each of us to perform.

I testify that Jesus Christ lives. This is His Church and kingdom on earth. Joseph Smith is the prophet of the Restoration. President Russell M. Nelson is the Lord's prophet on the earth today. He holds all the keys of the priesthood in The Church of Jesus Christ of Latter-day Saints. In the name of Jesus Christ, amen.

Notes

1. Russell M. Nelson, "My 2020 Invitation to You: Share the Message of the Restoration of the Savior's Gospel," Jan. 1, 2020, blog.ChurchofJesusChrist.org.

SATURDAY MORNING SESSION

2. *Teachings of Presidents of the Church: Joseph Smith* (2007), 512–13.
3. Mosiah 15:28.
4. Matthew 4:19.
5. *Discourses of Brigham Young,* sel. John A. Widtsoe (1954), 43–44.
6. Doctrine and Covenants 20:77.
7. Enos 1:4–8.

THE COMING FORTH OF THE BOOK OF MORMON

ELDER ULISSES SOARES
Of the Quorum of the Twelve Apostles

While meeting with the elders of the Church on one occasion, the Prophet Joseph Smith declared: "Take away the Book of Mormon, and the revelations, and where is our religion? We have none."[1] My dear brothers and sisters, following the First Vision, the miraculous coming forth of the Book of Mormon is the second fundamental milestone of the unfolding Restoration of the gospel of Jesus Christ in this dispensation. The Book of Mormon testifies of God's love for His children, of the Lord Jesus Christ's selfless and divine atoning sacrifice, and of His crowning ministry among the Nephites soon after His Resurrection.[2] It also testifies that the remnant of the house of Israel is to become one through His latter-day work and that they are not cast off forever.[3]

As we study the coming forth of this holy book of scripture in these latter days, we come to realize that the entire undertaking was miraculous—from the Prophet Joseph receiving the gold plates from a holy angel to its translation "by the gift and power of God,"[4] its preservation, and its publication by the hand of the Lord.

The coming forth of the Book of Mormon began long before Joseph Smith received the gold plates from the hands of the angel Moroni. Prophets of old prophesied about this sacred book's advent in our day.[5] Isaiah spoke of a sealed book, that when it would appear people would be contending over God's word. This circumstance would provide the context wherein God could perform His "marvellous work and a wonder," causing "the wisdom of their wise men [to] perish, and the understanding of their prudent men [to] be hid," while the meek would "increase their joy in the Lord, and the poor among men shall rejoice in the Holy One of Israel."[6] Ezekiel spoke about the stick of Judah (the Bible) and the stick of Ephraim (the Book of Mormon) being brought together as one. Both Ezekiel (in the Old Testament) and Lehi (in the Book of Mormon) indicate that they shall "grow together" to confound false doctrine, establish peace, and bring us to a knowledge of the covenants.[7]

In the evening of September 21, 1823, three and a half years after experiencing the First Vision, Joseph was visited three times by the angel Moroni, the last prophet of the Nephites in ancient America, as a result of his sincere prayers. During their visits that lasted through the night, Moroni told Joseph that God had a marvelous work for him to accomplish—the translation and publication to the world of the inspired words of ancient prophets of the American continent.[8] The next day, Joseph went to the place, not far from his home, where the plates were buried by Moroni at the end of his life, centuries earlier. There Joseph saw Moroni again, who instructed him to prepare himself to receive the plates in the future.

Over the next four years, on September 22 of each year, Joseph received additional instructions from Moroni regarding the knowledge about how the Lord's kingdom should be governed in the latter days. Joseph's preparation also included visits from the angels of God, thus unfolding the majesty and glory of the events that would take place in this dispensation.[9]

His marriage to Emma Hale in 1827 was part of that preparation. She played an important role in helping the Prophet throughout his life and ministry. In fact, in September 1827, Emma accompanied Joseph to the hill where the plates were hidden, and she waited for him as the angel Moroni delivered the record into Joseph's hands. Joseph received the promise that the plates would be preserved if he would devote all his efforts to keep them safe until they should be returned into the hands of Moroni.[10]

My dear fellow companions in the gospel, many of today's discoveries from ancient times occur during an archaeological excavation or even by accident during a construction project. Joseph Smith, however, was directed to the plates by an angel. That outcome by itself was a miracle.

The translation process of the Book of Mormon was also a miracle. This sacred ancient record was not "translated" in the traditional way that scholars would translate ancient texts by learning an ancient language. We ought to look at the process more like a "revelation" with the aid of physical instruments provided by the Lord, as opposed to a "translation" by one with knowledge of languages. Joseph Smith declared that through God's power he "translated the Book of Mormon from [hieroglyphs], the knowledge of which was lost to the world, in which wonderful event [he] stood alone, an unlearned youth, to combat the worldly wisdom and multiplied ignorance of eighteen centuries, with a new revelation."[11] The Lord's help in the translation of the plates—or revelation, so to speak—is also evident when considering the miraculously short time Joseph Smith took to translate them.[12]

Joseph's scribes testified of the power of God that was manifested while working on the translation of the Book of Mormon. Oliver Cowdery once said: "These were days never to be forgotten—to sit under the sound of a voice dictated by the inspiration of heaven, awakened the utmost gratitude of this bosom! Day after day I continued, uninterrupted, to write from his mouth, as he translated . . . 'The Book of Mormon.'"[13]

Historical sources reveal that from the moment Joseph obtained the plates in 1827, attempts were made to steal them from him. He noted that "the most strenuous exertions were used to get [the plates] from [him]" and that "every stratagem that could be invented was resorted to for that purpose."[14] Eventually Joseph and Emma were forced to move from Manchester, New York, to Harmony, Pennsylvania, to find a safe place to proceed with the work of translation, away from mobs and individuals who wanted to steal the plates.[15] As one historian notes: "Thus ended the first difficult phase of Joseph's guardianship over the plates. . . . Yet the record was safe, and in his struggles to preserve them Joseph no doubt had learned much about the ways of God and man that would serve him well in the time to come."[16]

While translating the Book of Mormon, Joseph learned that the Lord would choose witnesses to see the plates.[17] This is part of what the Lord Himself established when He said, "In the mouth of two or three witnesses every word may be established."[18] Oliver Cowdery,

David Whitmer, and Martin Harris, who were some of Joseph's initial companions in the establishment of God's marvelous work in this dispensation, were the first witnesses called to bear a special testimony of the Book of Mormon to the world. They testified that an angel, who came from the presence of the Lord, showed them the ancient record and that they saw the characters engraved in the plates. They also testified that they heard the voice of God from heaven declaring that the ancient record was translated by the gift and power of God. Then they were commanded to testify of it to the entire world.[19]

The Lord miraculously called another eight witnesses to see the gold plates for themselves and to be special witnesses of the truth and divinity of the Book of Mormon to the world. They testified that they saw and carefully examined the plates and their engraved characters. Even amid the adversities, persecutions, all kinds of difficulties, and even some of them later faltering in their faith, these eleven chosen Book of Mormon witnesses never denied their testimonies that they had seen the plates. Joseph Smith was not alone anymore with the knowledge of Moroni's visits and the gold plates.

Lucy Mack Smith recorded that her son arrived home overcome with joy after the witnesses were shown the plates. Joseph explained to his parents, "I feel as if I was relieved of a burden which was almost too heavy for me to bear, and it rejoices my soul, that I am not any longer to be entirely alone in the world."[20]

Joseph Smith faced much opposition in printing the Book of Mormon as its translation came to an end. He was able to convince a printer named Egbert B. Grandin in Palmyra, New York, to print it only after Martin Harris, in an act of great faith and sacrifice, mortgaged his farm as collateral for the printing costs. Due in part to the continuing opposition after the publication of the Book of Mormon, Martin Harris faithfully sold 151 acres (0.6 km^2) of his farm to pay off the publication costs. Through a revelation given to Joseph Smith, the Lord instructed Martin Harris to not covet his property and pay the printing cost for the book that "contains the truth and the word of God."[21] In March 1830 the first 5,000 copies of the Book of Mormon were published, and today more than 180 million copies have been printed in over a hundred languages.

The historical facts and the special witnesses of the Book of Mormon testify that its coming forth was indeed miraculous. Nevertheless, the power of this book is not based only in its magnificent history but on its powerful, unparalleled message that has changed countless lives—including mine!

I read the entire Book of Mormon for the first time when I was a young seminary student. As recommended by my teachers, I started reading it beginning with its introduction pages. The promise contained in the first pages of the Book of Mormon still echoes in my mind: "Ponder in [your] hearts . . . , and then . . . ask God [in faith] . . . in the name of Christ if the book is true. Those who pursue this course . . . will gain a testimony of its truth and divinity by the power of the Holy Ghost."[22]

With that promise in mind, earnestly seeking to know more about the truth of it, and in a spirit of prayer, I studied the Book of Mormon, little by little, as I completed the weekly assigned seminary lessons. I remember, like it was yesterday, that a warm feeling gradually began swelling in my soul and filling my heart, enlightening my understanding, and becoming more and more delightful, as described by Alma in his preaching the word of God to his people.[23] That feeling eventually turned into knowledge that took root in my heart and became the foundation of my testimony of the significant events and teachings found in this sacred book.

Through these and other priceless personal experiences, the Book of Mormon indeed became the keystone that sustains my faith in Jesus Christ and my testimony of the doctrine of His gospel. It became one of the pillars that testifies to me of Christ's divine atoning sacrifice. It became a shield throughout my life against the adversary's attempts to weaken my faith and instill disbelief in my mind and gives me courage to boldly declare my testimony of the Savior to the world.

My dear friends, my testimony of the Book of Mormon came line upon line[24] as a miracle to my heart. To this day, this testimony continues to grow as I continuously search, with a sincere heart, to more fully understand the word of God as contained in this extraordinary book of scripture.

To all who hear my voice today, I invite you to be part of the marvelous coming forth of the Book of Mormon in your own life. I promise you that as you prayerfully and consistently study its words, you can partake of its promises and rich blessings in your life. I reaffirm once more the promise that echoes through its pages: that if you "ask God, the Eternal Father, in the name of Christ, if these things are not true; and if ye shall ask with a sincere heart, with real intent, having faith in Christ," He mercifully "will manifest the truth of it unto you, by the power of the Holy Ghost."[25] I can assure you that He will give you the answer in a very personal way, as He has done for me and many others around the world. Your experience will be as glorious and sacred for you as Joseph Smith's experiences were for him, as well as for the first witnesses and for all who have sought to receive a witness of the integrity and trustworthiness of this sacred book.

I bear my witness that the Book of Mormon is indeed the word of God. I testify that this sacred record "puts forth the doctrines of the gospel, outlines the plan of salvation, and tells men what they must do to gain peace in this life and eternal salvation in the life to come."[26] I testify that the Book of Mormon is God's instrument to bring about the gathering of Israel in our day and to help people come to know His Son, Jesus Christ. I testify that God lives and loves us and His Son, Jesus Christ, is the Savior of the world, the chief cornerstone of our religion. I say these things in the sacred name of our Redeemer, our Master, and our Lord, even Jesus Christ, amen.

Notes
1. Joseph Smith, in "Minute Book 1," 44, josephsmithpapers.org; also at Church History Library, Salt Lake City; capitalization standardized.
2. See 3 Nephi 11–26.
3. See Ezekiel 37:21–28; 1 Nephi 13:34–41; 3 Nephi 20:46; 21:1–11; title page of the Book of Mormon.
4. Introduction to the Book of Mormon.
5. See Revelation 14:6–7; 1 Nephi 19:21.

6. Isaiah 29:14, 19; see also verses 11–13.
7. See Ezekiel 37:16–17; 2 Nephi 3:12.
8. See Joseph Smith—History 1:27–47; see also Doctrine and Covenants 27:5; Joseph Smith, "History, 1838–1856, volume A-1 [23 December 1805–30 August 1834]," 5, josephsmithpapers.org.
9. See Joseph Smith—History 1:54; see also Joseph Smith, "Church History," *Times and Seasons,* Mar. 1, 1842, 707, josephsmithpapers.org.
10. See Joseph Smith—History 1:59; *Teachings of Presidents of the Church: Joseph Smith* (2007), 57–59.
11. Joseph Smith, "History, 1838–1856, volume E-1 [1 July 1843–30 April 1844]," 1775, josephsmithpapers.org; also at Church History Library, Salt Lake City; punctuation standardized. See also Joseph Smith, "Letter to James Arlington Bennet, 13 November 1843," 1, josephsmithpapers.org; also at Church History Library, Salt Lake City.
12. See John W. Welch, "Timing the Translation of the Book of Mormon: 'Days [and Hours] Never to Be Forgotten,'" *BYU Studies,* vol. 57, no. 4 (2018), 11–50.
13. Oliver Cowdery, quoted in Joseph Smith—History 1:71, footnote; see also *Latter Day Saints' Messenger and Advocate,* Oct. 1834, 14.
14. Joseph Smith—History 1:60.
15. See Joseph Smith—History 1:60–62.
16. Andrew H. Hedges, "'All My Endeavors to Preserve Them': Protecting the Plates in Palmyra, 22 September–December 1827," *Journal of Book of Mormon Studies,* vol. 8, no. 2 (1999), 23.
17. See 2 Nephi 27:12–14; Ether 5:1–3.
18. Matthew 18:16.
19. See "The Testimony of Three Witnesses," Book of Mormon.
20. Joseph Smith, in Lucy Smith, *Biographical Sketches of Joseph Smith, the Prophet, and His Progenitors for Many Generations* (1880); see also "Lucy Mack Smith, History, 1845," 154, josephsmithpapers.org.
21. Doctrine and Covenants 19:26.
22. Introduction to the Book of Mormon; see also Moroni 10:3–5.
23. See Alma 32:41–43.
24. See 2 Nephi 28:30.
25. Moroni 10:4.
26. Introduction to the Book of Mormon.

COME UNTO CHRIST—
LIVING AS LATTER-DAY SAINTS

ELDER JOHN A. McCUNE
Of the Seventy

Thank you, Elder Soares, for your powerful and prophetic testimony of the Book of Mormon. Recently, I had the unique opportunity to hold a page of the original manuscript of the Book of Mormon. On this particular page, for the first time in this dispensation, these bold words of Nephi were recorded: "I will go and do the things which the Lord hath commanded, for I know that the Lord giveth no commandments unto the children of men, save he shall prepare a way for them that they may accomplish the thing which he commandeth them."[1]

As I held this page, I was filled with a profound appreciation for the efforts of the 23-year-old Joseph Smith, who translated the Book of Mormon by the "gift and power of God."[2] I also felt appreciation for the words of a young Nephi, who had been asked to perform a very difficult task in obtaining the plates of brass from Laban.

Nephi knew that if he continued to stay focused on the Lord, he would be successful in fulfilling what the Lord commanded him. He remained focused on the Savior throughout his life even though he suffered temptations, physical trials, and even the betrayal of some in his immediate family.

Nephi knew in whom He could trust.[3] Shortly after exclaiming, "O wretched man that I am! Yea, my heart sorroweth because of my flesh,"[4] Nephi stated, "My God hath been my support; he hath led me through mine afflictions in the wilderness; and he hath preserved me upon the waters of the great deep."[5]

As followers of Christ, we are not spared challenges and trials in our lives. We are often required to do difficult things that, if attempted alone, would be overwhelming and maybe impossible. As we accept the Savior's invitation to "come unto me,"[6] He will provide the support, comfort, and peace that are necessary, just as He did for Nephi and Joseph. Even in our deepest trials, we can feel the warm embrace of His love as we trust Him and accept His will. We can experience the joy reserved for His faithful disciples, for "Christ is joy."[7]

In 2014, while serving a full-time mission, our family experienced an unexpected turn of events. When riding down a steep hill on a longboard, our youngest son fell and sustained a life-threatening injury to his brain. As his situation deteriorated, medical personnel rushed him into emergency surgery.

Our family knelt on the floor of an otherwise empty hospital room, and we poured our hearts out to God. In the midst of this confusing and painful moment, we were filled with our Heavenly Father's love and peace.

We did not know what the future held or if we would see our son alive again. We did know very clearly that his life was in God's hands and the results, from an eternal perspective, would work out for his and our good. Through the gift of the Spirit, we were fully prepared to accept any outcome.

It was not easy! The accident resulted in a two-month hospital stay while we were presiding over 400 full-time missionaries. Our son experienced a significant loss of memory. His recovery included long and difficult physical, speech, and occupational therapy sessions. Challenges remain, but over time we have witnessed a miracle.

We understand clearly that not every trial we face will have a result we wish for. However, as we remain focused on Christ, we will feel peace and see God's miracles, whatever they may be, in His time and in His way.

There will be times when we will not be able to see any way that a current situation will end well and might even express, as Nephi, "My heart sorroweth because of my flesh."[8] There may be times that the only hope we have *is* in Jesus Christ. What a blessing to have that hope and trust in Him. Christ is the one who will always keep His promises. His rest is assured for all who come unto Him.[9]

Our leaders deeply desire all to feel the peace and comfort that come through trusting in and focusing on the Savior Jesus Christ.

Our living prophet, President Russell M. Nelson, has been

communicating the Lord's vision for the world and for members of Christ's Church: "Our message to the world is simple and sincere: we invite all of God's children on both sides of the veil to *come unto their Savior,* receive the blessings of the holy temple, have enduring joy, and qualify for eternal life."[10]

This invitation to "come unto Christ" has *specific* implications for Latter-day Saints.[11] As members of the Savior's Church, we have made covenants with Him and have become His spiritually begotten sons and daughters.[12] We have also been given the opportunity to labor with the Lord in inviting others to come unto Him.

As we labor with Christ, our most deeply focused efforts should be within our own homes. There will be times when family members and close friends will face challenges. The voices of the world, and maybe their own desires, might cause them to question truth. We should do everything we can to help them feel both the Savior's love and our love. I am reminded of the scripture verse that has become our beloved hymn "Love One Another," which teaches us, "By this shall . . . men know . . . ye are my disciples, if ye have love one to another."[13]

In our love for those who are questioning truth, the enemy of all joy might try to make us feel that we betray those we love if *we* ourselves continue to live the fulness of the gospel and teach its truths.

Our ability to help others come unto Christ or return to Christ will largely be determined by the example we set through our own personal commitment to stay on the covenant path.

If our true desire is to rescue those we love, we ourselves must stay firmly with Christ by embracing His Church and the fulness of His gospel.

In returning to Nephi's story, we know that Nephi's inclination to trust in the Lord was influenced by his parents' propensity to trust in the Lord and by their covenant-keeping example. This is beautifully exemplified in Lehi's vision of the tree of life. After partaking of the sweet and joyful fruit of the tree, Lehi "cast [his] eyes round about, that perhaps [he] might discover [his] family."[14] He saw Sariah, Sam, and Nephi standing "as if they knew not whither they should go."[15] Lehi then stated, "I beckoned unto them; and I also did say unto them with a loud voice that they should come unto me, and partake of the fruit."[16] Please note that Lehi did not leave the tree of life. He stayed spiritually with the Lord and invited his family to come where *he* was to partake of the fruit.

The adversary would entice some to leave the joy of the gospel by separating Christ's teachings from His Church. He would have us believe that we can stay firmly on the covenant path on our own, through our own spirituality, independent of His Church.

In these latter days, Christ's Church was restored in order to help Christ's covenant children stay on His covenant path.

In the Doctrine and Covenants we read, "Behold, this is my doctrine—whosoever repenteth and *cometh unto me,* the same *is* my church."[17]

Through Christ's Church, we are strengthened through our experiences as a community of Saints. We hear His voice through His prophets, seers, and revelators. Most importantly, through His Church we are provided with all the essential blessings of Christ's Atonement that can be realized only through participation in sacred ordinances.

The Church of Jesus Christ of Latter-day Saints is Christ's Church on the earth, restored in these latter days for the benefit of all of God's children.

I bear witness that as we come unto Christ and live as Latter-day Saints, we will be blessed with an added measure of His love, His joy, and His peace. Like Nephi, we can do difficult things and help others do the same, because we know in whom we can trust.[18] Christ is our light, our life, and our salvation.[19] In the name of Jesus Christ, amen.

Notes
1. 1 Nephi 3:7.
2. Title page of the Book of Mormon; see also introduction to the Book of Mormon.
3. See 2 Nephi 4:19.
4. 2 Nephi 4:17.
5. 2 Nephi 4:20.
6. Matthew 11:28.
7. Russell M. Nelson, "Joy and Spiritual Survival," *Ensign* or *Liahona,* Nov. 2016, 82.

8. 2 Nephi 4:17.
9. See Matthew 11:28–30.
10. Russell M. Nelson, "Let Us All Press On," *Ensign* or *Liahona,* May 2018, 118–19; emphasis added.
11. See Doctrine and Covenants 20:59.
12. See Mosiah 5:7.
13. John 13:35; see also "Love One Another," *Hymns,* no. 308.
14. 1 Nephi 8:13.
15. 1 Nephi 8:14.
16. 1 Nephi 8:15.
17. Doctrine and Covenants 10:67; emphasis added.
18. See 2 Nephi 4:19.
19. See Psalm 27:1.

A LIVING WITNESS OF THE LIVING CHRIST

BISHOP GÉRALD CAUSSÉ
Presiding Bishop

The central message of the Book of Mormon is to restore the true knowledge of the essential role of Jesus Christ in the salvation and exaltation of mankind.

On a sunny spring day in 2017, the open house for the Paris France Temple was well underway when one of the tour guides was approached by a man with a sorrowful expression on his face. He said he lived next to the temple and admitted he had been an active opponent of its construction. He related that one day as he was gazing out of his apartment window, he watched a large crane lower a statue of Jesus from the heavens and softly place it on the temple grounds. The man declared that this experience completely changed his feelings toward our Church. He realized we were followers of Jesus Christ and begged our forgiveness for the previous harm he might have caused.

The statue of the *Christus,* which adorns the grounds of the Paris Temple and other Church properties, testifies of our love for the Savior. The original marble statue is the work of the Danish artist Bertel Thorvaldsen, who sculpted it in 1820—the same year as the First Vision. The statue stands in stark contrast to most of the artistic renderings of that period, which largely portray the suffering Christ on the cross. Thorvaldsen's work presents the living Christ, who gained victory over death and, with open arms, invites all to come unto Him. Only the prints of the nails in His hands and feet and the wound in His side testify of the indescribable agony He endured to save all mankind.

Perhaps one reason we as members of The Church of Jesus Christ of Latter-day Saints love this statue is that it reminds us of the description given in the Book of Mormon of the Savior's appearance on the American continent:

"And behold, they saw a Man descending out of heaven; and

he was clothed in a white robe; and he came down and stood in the midst of them. . . .

"And it came to pass that he stretched forth his hand and spake unto the people, saying:

"Behold, I am Jesus Christ, . . .

" . . . I have drunk out of that bitter cup which the Father hath given me, and have glorified the Father in taking upon me the sins of the world."[1]

Then He invited each man, woman, and child to come forth and thrust their hands into His side and feel the prints of the nails in His hands and feet, thereby receiving a personal witness that He was indeed the long-awaited Messiah.[2]

This sublime scene is the climax of the Book of Mormon. The entire "good news" of the gospel is contained in this image of the Savior tenderly extending His "arms of mercy"[3] to invite each individual to come unto Him and receive the blessings of His Atonement.

The central message of the Book of Mormon is to restore the true knowledge of the essential role of Jesus Christ in the salvation and exaltation of mankind. This theme reverberates from the introductory page through the very last words of the last chapter. Through centuries of apostasy and spiritual confusion, the deeper meaning of what Christ did in Gethsemane and on Golgotha became lost or corrupted. How excited Joseph Smith must have felt when, as he was translating 1 Nephi, he discovered this marvelous promise: "These last records [the Book of Mormon] . . . shall establish the truth of the first [the Bible] . . . and shall make known the plain and precious things which have been taken away from them; and shall make known to all kindreds, tongues, and people, that the Lamb of God is the Son of the Eternal Father, and the Savior of the world; and that all men must come unto him, or they cannot be saved."[4]

Plain and precious truths about the Savior's Atonement resound throughout the Book of Mormon. As I list several of these truths, I invite you to reflect on how they have changed or could change your life.

The Atonement of Jesus Christ is a free gift offered to *all* who *have* lived, who *currently* live, and who *will* live on the earth.[5]

In addition to bearing the burden of our sins, the Christ took upon Himself our sorrows, infirmities, sufferings, and sicknesses and all the afflictions inherent in the mortal condition of man. There is no anguish, no pain or sadness that He did not suffer for us.[6]

The atoning sacrifice of the Savior allows us to overcome the negative consequences of Adam's Fall, including physical death. Because of Christ, all of God's children born on this earth, regardless of their righteousness, will experience the reuniting of their spirits and bodies through the power of the Resurrection[7] and return to Him to "be judged . . . according to [their] works."[8]

In contrast, receiving the full blessings of the Savior's Atonement is conditioned upon our diligence[9] in living the "doctrine of Christ."[10] In his dream, Lehi saw the "strait and narrow path"[11] that leads to the tree of life. Its fruit, which represents the love of God as expressed through the exquisite blessings of Christ's Atonement, "is most precious and most desirable . . . [and] is the greatest of all the gifts of God."[12] In order to access this fruit, we must exercise faith in Jesus Christ, repent, "hearken unto the word of God,"[13] receive essential ordinances, and keep sacred covenants until the end of our lives.[14]

Through His Atonement, Jesus Christ not only washes away our sins, but He also provides *enabling* power through which His disciples may "[put] off the natural man,"[15] progress "line upon line,"[16] and increase in holiness[17] so that one day they might become perfect beings in the image of Christ,[18] qualified to live again with God[19] and inherit all the blessings of the kingdom of heaven.[20]

Another comforting truth contained in the Book of Mormon is that, although infinite and universal in its reach, the Lord's Atonement is a remarkably personal and intimate gift, suited to each of us individually.[21] Just as Jesus invited each one of the Nephite disciples to feel His wounds, He died for each one of us, personally, as if you or I were the only person on earth. He extends to us a personal invitation to come unto Him and draw upon the marvelous blessings of His Atonement.[22]

The personal nature of Christ's Atonement becomes even more real as we consider the examples of remarkable men and women in the Book of Mormon. Among them are Enos, Alma, Zeezrom, King Lamoni and his wife, and the people of King Benjamin. Their conversion stories and vibrant testimonies provide a living witness of how our hearts can be changed and our lives transformed through the Lord's infinite goodness and mercy.[23]

The prophet Alma asked his people this burning question. He said, "If ye have experienced a change of heart, and if ye have felt to sing the song of redeeming love, I would ask, can ye feel so *now?*"[24] This question is vital today, because as disciples of the Lord, we need His redeeming power to accompany us, motivate us, and change us each and every day.

Alma's question could also be rephrased to ask, when was the last time you felt the sweet influence of the Savior's Atonement in your life? This happens when you feel an "exquisite and sweet" joy[25] come over you that bears witness to your soul that your sins are forgiven; or when painful trials suddenly become lighter to bear; or when your heart is softened and you are able to express forgiveness to someone who has hurt you. Or it may be each time you notice your capacity to love and serve others has increased or that the process of sanctification is making you a different person, patterned after the Savior's example.[26]

I bear witness that all these experiences are real and are evidence that lives can be changed through faith in Jesus Christ and His Atonement. The Book of Mormon clarifies and expands our knowledge of this supernal gift. As you study this book, you will hear the voice of the living Christ inviting you to come unto Him. I promise that if you accept this invitation and pattern your life after His example, His redemptive influence will come into your life. Through the power of the Holy Ghost, the Savior will transform you day after day "until the perfect day"[27] when you will, as He declared, "see my face and know that I am."[28] In the name of Jesus Christ, amen.

Notes

1. 3 Nephi 11:8–11.
2. See 3 Nephi 11:14–15.
3. Alma 5:33.
4. 1 Nephi 13:40.
5. See 2 Nephi 9:21; 26:24–27; Mosiah 3:13.
6. See Alma 7:11–12.
7. See 2 Nephi 10:25.
8. Mosiah 3:24; see also 2 Nephi 2:4, 10, 26; 9:6–7, 12–13, 15, 22; Mosiah 3:12; 16:7–8; Alma 11:41–44; 42:6–8, 23; Helaman 14:16; Mormon 9:12.
9. See 2 Nephi 9:21; Mosiah 3:12; Helaman 5:11; 14:18.
10. 2 Nephi 31:21; see also 3 Nephi 27:20–21.
11. 1 Nephi 8:20.
12. 1 Nephi 15:36.
13. 1 Nephi 15:24.
14. See 2 Nephi 31.
15. Mosiah 3:19.
16. 2 Nephi 28:30.
17. See Mosiah 3:19.
18. See 3 Nephi 27:27; Moroni 10:32–33.
19. See 2 Nephi 2:8; Mosiah 2:41.
20. See Alma 11:37.
21. See 2 Nephi 9:21.
22. See Omni 1:26; Alma 5:33; Moroni 10:32–33.
23. See Enos 1; Mosiah 5; Alma 12; 18–19; 36.
24. Alma 5:26; emphasis added.
25. Alma 36:21.
26. See Mosiah 3:19.
27. Doctrine and Covenants 50:24.
28. Doctrine and Covenants 93:1.

CONSIDER THE GOODNESS AND GREATNESS OF GOD

ELDER DALE G. RENLUND
Of the Quorum of the Twelve Apostles

Throughout time, even and especially during difficult times, prophets have encouraged us to remember the greatness of God and to consider what He has done for us as individuals, as families, and as a people.[1] This direction is found throughout the scriptures but is notably prominent in the Book of Mormon. The title page explains that one of the Book of Mormon's purposes is "to show unto the remnant of the house of Israel what great things the Lord hath done for their fathers."[2] The Book of Mormon's conclusion includes Moroni's appeal: "Behold, I would exhort you that when ye shall read these things . . . that ye would remember how merciful the Lord hath been unto the children of men . . . and ponder it in your hearts."[3]

The consistency of pleas from prophets to reflect on the goodness of God is striking.[4] Our Heavenly Father wants us to recall His and His Beloved Son's goodness, not for Their own gratification but for the influence such remembrance has on us. By considering Their kindness, our perspective and understanding are enlarged. By reflecting on Their compassion, we become more humble, prayerful, and steadfast.

A poignant experience with a former patient shows how gratitude for generosity and compassion can transform us. In 1987, I became acquainted with Thomas Nielson, a remarkable man who needed a heart transplant. He was 63 years old and lived in Logan, Utah, in the United States. Following military service during World War II, he married Donna Wilkes in the Logan Utah Temple. He became an energetic and successful brick mason. In later years he especially enjoyed working with his oldest grandchild, Jonathan, during school vacations. The two developed a special bond, in part because Tom saw much of himself in Jonathan.

Tom found waiting for a donor heart frustrating. He was not a particularly patient man. He had always been able to set and achieve goals through hard work and sheer determination. Struggling with heart failure, with his life on hold, Tom sometimes asked me what I was doing to speed up the process. Jokingly, he suggested avenues I could pursue that would make a donor heart available to him sooner.

One joyous yet dreadful day, an ideal donor heart became available for Tom. The size and blood type were a match, and the donor was young, just 16 years old. The donor heart belonged to Jonathan, Tom's beloved grandson. Earlier that day, Jonathan had been fatally injured when the car in which he was riding was struck by a passing train.

When I visited Tom and Donna in the hospital, they were distraught. It is hard to imagine what they were going through, knowing that Tom's life could be extended by using their grandson's heart. At first, they refused to consider the proffered heart from Jonathan's grieving parents, their daughter and son-in-law. Tom and Donna knew, though, that Jonathan was brain dead, and came to understand that their prayers for a donor heart for Tom had not caused Jonathan's accident. No, Jonathan's heart was a gift that could bless Tom in his time of need. They recognized that something good might come out of this tragedy and decided to proceed.

The transplant procedures went well. Afterward, Tom was a different man. The change went beyond improved health or even gratitude. He told me that he reflected every morning on Jonathan, on his daughter and son-in-law, on the gift he had received, and on what that gift had entailed. Even though his innate good humor and grit were still readily apparent, I observed that Tom was more solemn, thoughtful, and kindhearted.

Tom lived an additional 13 years after the transplant, years he otherwise would not have had. His obituary stated that these years allowed him to touch the lives of his family and others with generosity and love. He was a private benefactor and an example of optimism and determination.

Much like Tom, each of us has received gifts that we could not provide for ourselves, gifts from our Heavenly Father and His

Beloved Son, including redemption through the atoning sacrifice of Jesus Christ.[5] We have received life in this world; we will receive physical life in the hereafter, and eternal salvation and exaltation—if we choose it—all because of Heavenly Father and Jesus Christ.

Every time we use, benefit from, or even think of these gifts, we ought to consider the sacrifice, generosity, and compassion of the givers. Reverence for the givers does more than just make us grateful. Reflecting on Their gifts can and should transform us.

One remarkable transformation was that of Alma the Younger. As Alma was "going about rebelling against God,"[6] an angel appeared. With "a voice of thunder,"[7] the angel chastised Alma for persecuting the Church and "stealing away the hearts of the people."[8] The angel added this admonition: "Go, and remember the captivity of thy fathers . . . ; and remember how great things [God] has done for them."[9] Of all possible exhortations, that was what the angel emphasized.

Alma repented and remembered. He later shared the angel's admonition with his son Helaman. Alma counseled, "I would that ye should do as I have done, in remembering the captivity of our fathers; for they were in bondage, and none could deliver them except it was the God of Abraham, . . . Isaac, and . . . Jacob; and he surely did deliver them in their afflictions."[10] Alma said simply, "I do put my trust in him."[11] Alma understood that by remembering deliverance from bondage and support during "trials and troubles of every kind," we come to know God and the surety of His promises.[12]

Few of us have an experience as dramatic as Alma's, yet our transformation can be equally profound. The Savior pledged anciently:

"A new heart also will I give you, and a new spirit will I put within you: and I will take away the stony heart . . . , and I will give you an heart of flesh.

"And I will put my spirit within you. . . .

" . . . And ye shall be my people, and I will be your God."[13]

The resurrected Savior told the Nephites how this transformation begins. He identified a pivotal feature in Heavenly Father's plan when He said:

"And my Father sent me that I might be lifted up upon the cross; and after that I had been lifted up upon the cross, that I might *draw* all men unto me. . . .

"And for this cause have I been lifted up; therefore, according to the power of the Father I will *draw* all men unto me."[14]

What does it take for you to be drawn to the Savior? Consider Jesus Christ's submission to His Father's will, His victory over death, His taking upon Himself your sins and mistakes, His receiving power from the Father to make intercession for you, and His ultimate redemption of you.[15] Are these things not sufficient to draw you to Him? They are for me. Jesus Christ "stands with open arms, hoping and willing to heal, forgive, cleanse, strengthen, purify, and sanctify [you and me]."[16]

These truths should give us a new heart and prompt us to choose to follow Heavenly Father and Jesus Christ. Yet even new hearts may be "prone to wander, . . . prone to leave the God [we] love."[17] To fight this tendency, we need to reflect every day on the gifts we have received and on what they entailed. King Benjamin counseled, "I would that ye should remember, and always retain in remembrance, the greatness of God . . . and his goodness and long-suffering towards you."[18] If we do so, we qualify for remarkable heavenly blessings.

Reflecting on God's goodness and mercy helps us become more spiritually receptive. In turn, increased spiritual sensitivity allows us to come to know the truth of all things by the power of the Holy Ghost.[19] This includes a testimony of the truthfulness of the Book of Mormon; knowing that Jesus is the Christ, our personal Savior and Redeemer; and accepting that His gospel has been restored in these latter days.[20]

When we remember the greatness of our Heavenly Father and Jesus Christ and what They have done for us, we will not take Them for granted, just as Tom did not take Jonathan's heart for granted. In a joyful and reverent way, Tom remembered each day the tragedy that brought him extended life. In the exuberance of knowing that we can be saved and exalted, we need to remember that salvation and exaltation came at a great cost.[21] We can be reverently joyful as we realize that without Jesus Christ, we are doomed, but with Him, we can receive the greatest gift Heavenly Father can give.[22] Indeed, this reverence allows us to enjoy the promise "of eternal life in this world" and eventually receive "eternal life . . . even immortal glory" in the world to come.[23]

When we consider the goodness of our Heavenly Father and Jesus Christ, our trust in Them increases. Our prayers change because we know God is our Father and we are His children. We seek not to change His will but to align our will with His and secure for ourselves blessings that He wants to grant, conditioned on our asking for them.[24] We yearn to be more meek, more pure, more steadfast, more Christlike.[25] These changes qualify us for additional heavenly blessings.

By acknowledging that every good thing comes from Jesus Christ, we will communicate our faith more effectively to others.[26] We will have courage when confronted with seemingly impossible tasks and circumstances.[27] We will strengthen our resolve to keep the covenants we have made to follow the Savior.[28] We will be filled with the love of God, want to help those in need without being judgmental, love our children and raise them in righteousness, retain a remission of our sins, and always rejoice.[29] These are the remarkable fruits of remembering God's goodness and mercy.

In contrast, the Savior warned, "In nothing doth man offend God, or against none is his wrath kindled, save those who confess not his hand in all things."[30] I do not think that God is insulted when we forget Him. Rather, I think He is deeply disappointed. He knows that we have deprived ourselves of the opportunity to draw closer to Him by remembering Him and His goodness. We then miss out on Him drawing nearer to us and the specific blessings He has promised.[31]

I invite you to remember each day the greatness of Heavenly Father and Jesus Christ and what They have done for you. Let your consideration of Their goodness more firmly bind your wandering heart to Them.[32] Ponder Their compassion, and you will be blessed with added spiritual sensitivity and become more Christlike. Contemplating Their empathy will help you "hold out faithful to the end," until you "are received into heaven" to "dwell with God in a state of never-ending happiness."[33]

Our Heavenly Father, referring to His Beloved Son, said, "Hear Him!"[34] As you act on those words and listen to Him, remember, joyfully and reverently, that the Savior loves to restore what you cannot restore; He loves to heal wounds you cannot heal; He loves to fix what has been irreparably broken;[35] He compensates for any unfairness inflicted on you;[36] and He loves to permanently mend even shattered hearts.[37]

As I have reflected on gifts from our Heavenly Father and from Jesus Christ, I have come to know of Their infinite love and Their incomprehensible compassion for all Heavenly Father's children.[38] This knowledge has changed me, and it will change you too. In the name of Jesus Christ, amen.

Notes

1. See, for instance, Abraham 2:16; Exodus 13:3; Joshua 4:6–9; 1 Samuel 7:11–12.
2. Title page of the Book of Mormon.
3. Moroni 10:3.
4. See, for example, Deuteronomy 6:12; 11:18; Joshua 4:21–24; 1 Samuel 7:12; Romans 2:4; 11:22; 2 Nephi 9:10; 33:14; Jacob 1:7; Mosiah 5:3; 25:10; 27:22; Alma 34:4; Helaman 12:2; 3 Nephi 4:33; 18:11–12; Mormon 2:13; Doctrine and Covenants 133:52; 138:2.
5. See Isaiah 53:3–12; Luke 22:44; John 3:16; Galatians 2:20; Mosiah 3:5–11; Alma 7:10–13; Doctrine and Covenants 19:16–19.
6. Mosiah 27:11.
7. Mosiah 27:11.
8. Mosiah 27:9; see also verse 13.
9. Mosiah 27:16.
10. Alma 36:2.
11. Alma 36:27.
12. See Alma 36:27–29.
13. Ezekiel 36:26–28.
14. 3 Nephi 27:14–15; emphasis added. See also John 12:32; 2 Nephi 26:24.
15. See Mosiah 15:7–9; Revelation 21:4.
16. Russell M. Nelson, "We Can Do Better and Be Better," *Ensign* or *Liahona*, May 2019, 67.
17. "Come, Thou Fount of Every Blessing," *Hymns* (1948), no. 70.
18. Mosiah 4:11; see also Alma 36:2, 28–29; Ether 7:27; 10:2; Moroni 9:25.
19. See Moroni 10:4–5.
20. See title page and introduction to the Book of Mormon.
21. See Doctrine and Covenants 19:18–19.
22. See Doctrine and Covenants 14:7.
23. Moses 6:59; see also Alma 36:28.
24. See Bible Dictionary, "Prayer."
25. See "More Holiness Give Me," *Hymns,* no. 131.

26. See Philemon 1:6.
27. See 1 Samuel 17:37; 1 Nephi 4:2.
28. See Alma 5:6, 13, 26–28.
29. See Mosiah 4:11–26.
30. Doctrine and Covenants 59:21.
31. See Doctrine and Covenants 88:63–64.
32. See "Come, Thou Fount of Every Blessing."
33. Mosiah 2:41.
34. See Matthew 17:5; Mark 9:7; Luke 9:35; 3 Nephi 11:7; Joseph Smith—History 1:17.
35. See Boyd K. Packer, "The Brilliant Morning of Forgiveness," *Ensign,* Nov. 1995, 19–20.
36. See Revelation 21:4.
37. See Psalm 147:3.
38. See 2 Nephi 26:33.

THE POWER OF THE BOOK OF MORMON IN CONVERSION

ELDER BENJAMIN M. Z. TAI
Of the Seventy

After reviewing the report from a recent physical examination, I learned that I needed to make some lifestyle adjustments. To help me, my doctor prescribed a nutrition and exercise plan, which, if I chose to follow it, would transform me into a healthier person.

If we each underwent a spiritual examination, what would we learn about ourselves? What adjustments would our spiritual physician prescribe? For us to become who we need to be, it is essential that we know what to do and do what we know.

Jesus Christ is the Master Physician.[1] Through His Atonement, He binds up our wounds, takes upon Himself our infirmities, and heals our broken hearts.[2] Through His grace our weakness can become strong.[3] He invites us to follow Him[4] by learning of Him, listening to His words, and walking in the meekness of His Spirit.[5] He has promised to help us[6] in this lifelong process of conversion, which transforms us and brings everlasting joy.[7]

The Savior has given us the Book of Mormon as a powerful tool to aid in conversion. The Book of Mormon provides spiritual nutrition, prescribes a plan of action, and connects us with the Holy Spirit. Written for us,[8] it contains the word of God in plainness[9] and tells us of our identity, purpose, and destiny.[10] With the Bible, the Book of Mormon testifies of Jesus Christ[11] and teaches how we can know truth and become like Him.

Brother Saw Polo was 58 years old when he was introduced to the restored gospel of Jesus Christ. When I met him, he had been serving as a branch president for several years, but I learned that he had never read the Book of Mormon because it was not yet available in his native Burmese. When I asked him how he knew that the book was true without having read it, he replied that he had studied the *Book of Mormon Stories* picture book every day by looking at the illustrations, using a dictionary to translate the English words, and taking careful notes of what he learned. He explained, "Every time I studied, I would pray about what I learned, and I would feel peace and joy, my mind would be clear, and my heart would be soft. I felt the Holy Ghost testifying to me that it was true. I know that the Book of Mormon is the word of God."

Like Brother Saw Polo, each of us can study the Book of Mormon according to our circumstances. As we desire to believe and ponder its teachings in our hearts, we can ask God in faith if the teachings are true.[12] If we are sincere in our desire to know and have real intent to act, He will answer us in our hearts through the Holy Ghost. It is by the power of the Holy Ghost that we will know the truth of all things.[13] When we obtain a divine witness of the Book of Mormon, we will also know by the same power that Jesus Christ is the Savior of the world, that Joseph Smith is His prophet, and that The Church of Jesus Christ of Latter-day Saints is His restored Church.[14]

As a young man beginning my missionary service, I boarded an airplane headed to Australia. Feeling very alone, anxious, and inadequate but having committed to serve, I desperately needed reassurance that what I believed in was true. I prayed and read my scriptures earnestly, but as the flight progressed, my self-doubt intensified and my physical condition deteriorated. After I had been struggling for several hours, a flight attendant walked down the aisle and stopped next to my seat. He took the Book of Mormon I was reading from my hands. He looked at the cover and said, "That's a great book!" then handed the book back to me and kept walking. I never saw him again.

While his words echoed in my ears, I distinctly heard and felt in my heart, "I am here, and I know where you are. Just do your best, for I will take care of the rest." On that airplane above the Pacific Ocean, I received a personal witness through my study of the Book of Mormon and the promptings of the Holy Spirit that my Savior knew who I was and that the gospel was true.

Elder David A. Bednar taught: "Knowing that the gospel is true is the essence of a testimony. Consistently being true to the gospel is the essence of conversion."[15] Conversion requires us to be "doers of the word, and not hearers only."[16] The Lord's action plan for us—the doctrine of Christ—is taught most clearly in the Book of Mormon.[17] It includes:

First, *exercising* faith in Jesus Christ by *trusting* Him, *keeping* His commandments, and *knowing* that He will help us.[18]

Second, *repenting* daily of our shortcomings and *experiencing* joy and peace when He forgives us.[19] Repentance requires us to *forgive* others[20] and helps us to move forward. The Savior has promised to forgive us as often as we repent.[21]

Third, *making and keeping* covenants with God through ordinances such as baptism. This will keep us on the covenant path that leads to Him.[22]

Fourth, *receiving* the gift of the Holy Ghost. This gift allows us the constant companionship of one who sanctifies, comforts, and guides us.[23]

And fifth, *enduring* to the end by *pressing forward* steadfastly while *feasting* daily upon the word of Christ.[24] By feasting from the Book of Mormon and holding fast to its teachings, we can overcome temptations and receive guidance and protection throughout our lives.[25]

By consistently applying the doctrine of Christ in our lives, we will overcome inertia that impedes change and fear that foils action. We will receive personal revelation, for the Holy Ghost "will *show* unto you all things what ye should do,"[26] and "the words of Christ will *tell* you all things what ye should do."[27]

For 20 years, Brother Huang Juncong struggled with alcohol, cigarettes, and compulsive gambling. When introduced to Jesus Christ and His restored gospel, Brother Huang desired to change for the sake of his young family. His greatest challenge was smoking. A heavy chain-smoker, he had tried to quit many times unsuccessfully. One day these words from the Book of Mormon lodged in his mind: "with a sincere heart, with real intent."[28] Though previous attempts had failed, he felt perhaps he could change with help from Heavenly Father and Jesus Christ.

The full-time missionaries united their faith with his and provided an action plan of practical interventions, along with heavy doses of prayer and studying the word of God. With sincerity and real intent, Brother Huang acted with faithful determination and found that as he focused more on the new habits he wished to develop, such as studying the Book of Mormon, he focused less on the habits he wanted to lose.

Recalling his experience from 15 years ago, he remarked, "I don't remember when exactly I quit smoking, but as I tried hard every day to do the things I knew I needed to do to invite the Spirit of the Lord into my life and kept doing them, I was no longer attracted to cigarettes and have not been since." Through applying the teachings of the Book of Mormon, Brother Huang's life has been transformed, and he has become a better husband and father.

President Russell M. Nelson has promised: "As you prayerfully study the Book of Mormon *every day,* you will make better decisions—*every day.* I promise that as you ponder what you study, the windows of heaven will open, and you will receive answers to your own questions and direction for your own life. I promise that as you daily immerse yourself in the Book of Mormon, you can be immunized against the evils of the day, even the gripping plague of pornography and other mind-numbing addictions."[29]

Dear friends, the Book of Mormon is the word of God, and we will draw nearer to Him if we study it.[30] As we experiment upon its words, we will obtain a witness of its truthfulness.[31] As we consistently live according to its teachings, we will have "no more desire to do evil."[32] Our heart, countenance, and nature will be transformed to become more like the Savior.[33] I share my sure witness that Jesus is the Christ, our Savior, Redeemer, and Friend. In the name of Jesus Christ, amen.

Notes

1. See Mark 2:17.
2. See Psalm 147:3; Isaiah 53:4; Matthew 8:17.
3. See 2 Nephi 25:23; Jacob 4:7; Ether 12:27.
4. See Matthew 19:21; Mark 10:21; Luke 18:22; 2 Nephi 31:10.
5. See Doctrine and Covenants 19:23.

SATURDAY AFTERNOON SESSION

6. See Isaiah 41:10.
7. See Mosiah 2:41; 3:19; 5:2.
8. See 2 Nephi 25:8, 21–22; Mormon 7:1; 8:35.
9. See 2 Nephi 25:7; 31:2–3.
10. See 2 Nephi 2:25; Alma 40.
11. See Isaiah 29:4, 11–18; Ezekiel 37:16–21; 2 Corinthians 13:1; 1 Nephi 13:38–42; 2 Nephi 3:12; 25:26.
12. See Alma 32:26–43.
13. See Moroni 10:3–5.
14. See introduction to the Book of Mormon.
15. David A. Bednar, "Converted unto the Lord," *Ensign* or *Liahona,* Nov. 2012, 109.
16. James 1:22.
17. See 2 Nephi 31; 3 Nephi 11:31–40; 27:13–22.
18. See 1 Nephi 3:7; Moroni 7:33.
19. See Mosiah 4:3.
20. See Matthew 18:21–35; Mark 11:25–26; Luke 6:37; 3 Nephi 13:14–15; Doctrine and Covenants 64:10; 82:1.
21. See Mosiah 26:30; Moroni 6:8.
22. See 2 Nephi 31:17–18.
23. See 1 Nephi 10:19; 2 Nephi 33:1; 3 Nephi 11:32; 28:11; Moroni 6:4.
24. See 2 Nephi 31:20.
25. See 1 Nephi 15:24.
26. 2 Nephi 32:5; emphasis added.
27. 2 Nephi 32:3; emphasis added.
28. Moroni 10:4.
29. Russell M. Nelson, "The Book of Mormon: What Would Your Life Be Like without It?" *Ensign* or *Liahona,* Nov. 2017, 62–63.
30. The Prophet Joseph Smith said of the Book of Mormon, "A man would get nearer to God by abiding by its precepts, than by any other book" (introduction to the Book of Mormon).
31. See Jacob 6:7; Alma 32:26–43.
32. Alma 19:33.
33. See 2 Corinthians 5:17; Mosiah 3:19; 5:2; Alma 5:14, 19.

A GOOD FOUNDATION AGAINST THE TIME TO COME

ELDER GARY E. STEVENSON
Of the Quorum of the Twelve Apostles

History of the Salt Lake Temple

Let's travel back to a hot afternoon on July 24, 1847, around 2:00 p.m. Following an arduous 111-day journey with 148 members of the Church who comprised the first party to head west, Brigham Young, then President of the Quorum of the Twelve Apostles, sick and weak from mountain fever, entered the Salt Lake Valley.

Two days later, while recovering from his illness, Brigham Young led several members of the Quorum of the Twelve Apostles and others on an exploring expedition. William Clayton recorded, "About three-quarters of a mile north of the camp, we arrived on a beautiful table of land, level and nicely sloping to the west."[1]

While surveying the spot with the group, Brigham Young suddenly stopped and stuck his cane in the ground, exclaiming, "Here shall stand the Temple of our God." One of his companions was Elder Wilford Woodruff, who said this statement "went through [him] like lightning," and he drove a branch into the ground to mark the spot made by President Young's cane. Forty acres (16 ha) were selected for the temple, and it was decided that the city should be laid out "perfectly square North & South, east & west" with the temple being the center spot.[2]

At general conference in April 1851, members of the Church voted unanimously to sustain a motion to build a temple "to the name of the Lord."[3] Two years later, on February 14, 1853, the site was dedicated by Heber C. Kimball in a public ceremony attended by several thousand Saints, and ground was broken for the foundation of the Salt Lake Temple. A few months later, on April 6, the massive cornerstones of the temple were laid and dedicated with elaborate ceremonies that included a color guard and bands and a procession led by Church leaders from the old tabernacle to the temple site, where remarks and prayers were offered at each of the four stones.[4]

At the groundbreaking ceremony, President Young recalled that he had seen a vision when he first set foot upon the ground as they surveyed the valley floor, stating, "I knew [then], just as well as I now know, that this was the ground on which to erect a temple—it was before me."[5]

Ten years later, Brigham Young offered the following prophetic insight at general conference in October 1863: "I want to see [the] temple built in a manner that it will endure through the millennium. This is not the only temple we shall build; there will be hundreds of them built and dedicated to the Lord. This temple will be known as the first temple built in the mountains by the Latter Day Saints. . . . I want that temple . . . to stand as a proud monument of the faith, perseverance and industry of the saints of God in the mountains."[6]

In reviewing this brief history, I am in awe of the seership of Brigham Young—first, his ensuring that, to the extent possible and, using construction methods available at that time and place, the Salt Lake Temple would be built in a manner to endure throughout the Millennium and, second, his prophesying of the growth of future temples worldwide, *even to number them in the hundreds.*

Salt Lake Temple Renovation

Like Brigham Young, our prophet of today looks over the Salt Lake Temple and all others with great care. Through the years, the First Presidency has, from time to time, counseled the Presiding Bishopric to ensure that the foundation of the Salt Lake Temple is solid. When I served in the Presiding Bishopric, at the request of the First Presidency, we did an overall facility review of the Salt Lake Temple, including an evaluation of the most recent advancements in seismic design and construction techniques.

Here are portions of the review provided to the First Presidency at that time: "In the design and construction of the Salt Lake Temple, the best engineering, skilled labor, construction materials, furnishings, and other period-available resources were used. Since its dedication in 1893, the temple has stood firm and served as a beacon of faith [and] hope and as a light unto the people. Great care has been taken to operate, clean, and maintain the temple in good condition. The granite exterior and interior floor joists and support beams are in good condition. Recent studies confirm that the location chosen by Brigham Young for the temple has very good soils and excellent compaction qualities."[7]

The review concluded that normal repairs and improvements were needed to renew and update the temple, including the exterior deck and surface areas, obsolete utility systems, and baptistry areas. However, consideration of a separate, more comprehensive seismic upgrade beginning from the temple foundation on upward was also recommended.

The Temple Foundation

As you may recall, President Brigham Young himself was involved in great detail in the construction of the original temple foundation, which has served the temple well since its completion 127 years ago. The newly proposed seismic upgrade package for the temple would utilize base isolation technology, which was not even imagined at the time of its construction. This is considered the latest, most state-of-the-art engineering for earthquake protection.

This technology, recent in its development, begins at the very foundation of the temple, providing a robust defense against damage from an earthquake. In essence, it structurally strengthens the temple to stand steadfast, even as the earth and environment around it undergo an earthshaking seismic event.

The temple renovation that would employ this technology was announced by the First Presidency last year. Under the direction of the Presiding Bishopric, construction commenced a few months ago, in January 2020. It is estimated to be completed in approximately four years.

SATURDAY AFTERNOON SESSION

Ensuring Your Personal Foundation

As I contemplate the next four years of the life of this beautiful, noble, exalted, and awe-inspiring Salt Lake Temple, I envision it more as a time of *renewal* rather than a time of closure! In a similar way, we might ask ourselves, "How could this extensive renewal of the Salt Lake Temple inspire us to undergo our own spiritual *renewal, reconstruction, rebirth, revitalization, or restoration?*"

An introspective look may reveal that we too and our families could benefit from our doing some needed maintenance and renovation work, even a seismic upgrade! We might start such a process by asking:

"What does my foundation look like?"

"What comprises the thick-walled, stable, strong cornerstones that are part of my personal foundation, upon which my testimony rests?"

"What are the foundational elements of my spiritual and emotional character that will allow me and my family to remain steadfast and immovable, even to withstand the earthshaking and tumultuous seismic events that will surely take place in our lives?"

These events, similar to an earthquake, are often difficult to predict and come in various levels of intensity—wrestling with questions or doubt, facing affliction or adversity, working through personal offenses with Church leaders, members, doctrine, or policy. The best defense against these lies in our spiritual foundation.

What might spiritual cornerstones of our personal and family lives be? They may be the simple, plain, and precious principles of gospel living—family prayer; scripture study, including the Book of Mormon; temple attendance; and gospel learning through *Come, Follow Me* and home evening. Other helpful resources to strengthen your spiritual foundation may include the Articles of Faith, the family proclamation, and "The Living Christ."

For me, the principles included in the questions discussed as part of receiving a temple recommend serve as a strong basis for a spiritual foundation—particularly the first four questions. I see them as spiritual cornerstones.

We, of course, are familiar with these questions, as President Russell M. Nelson read them to us one by one in the last general conference.

Do you have faith in and a testimony of God, the Eternal Father; His Son, Jesus Christ; and the Holy Ghost?

Do you have a testimony of the Atonement of Jesus Christ and of His role as your Savior and Redeemer?

Do you have a testimony of the Restoration of the gospel of Jesus Christ?

Do you sustain the President of The Church of Jesus Christ of Latter-day Saints as the prophet, seer, and revelator and as the only person on the earth authorized to exercise all priesthood keys?[8]

Can you see how you might consider these questions as valuable elements in your personal foundation to help you build and reinforce it? Paul taught the Ephesians of a church which was "built upon the foundation of the apostles and prophets, Jesus Christ himself being the chief corner stone; in whom all the building fitly framed together groweth unto an holy temple in the Lord."[9]

One of the greatest joys of my life is becoming acquainted with and inspired by members of the Church all over the world who are living exemplars of faith in Jesus Christ and His gospel. They have strong personal foundations that allow them to withstand seismic events with steady understanding, despite their heartache and pain.

To display this on a more personal level, I recently spoke at the funeral of a beautiful, vibrant young wife and mother (also a family friend of ours). She was a scrappy Division 1 soccer player when she met and married her dental student husband. They were blessed with a beautiful, precocious daughter. She valiantly battled with various forms of cancer for six challenging years. Despite the ever-present emotional and physical distress that she experienced, she trusted in her loving Heavenly Father and was often quoted widely by her social media followers for her famous saying: "God is in the details."

On one of her social media posts, she wrote that someone had asked her, "How do you still have faith with all the heartache that surrounds you?" She replied firmly with these words: "Because faith is what gets me through these dark times. Having faith doesn't mean nothing bad is going to happen. Having faith allows me to believe that there will be light again. And that light will be even brighter because I have walked through the dark. As much darkness as I have witnessed over the years, I have witnessed far more light. I have seen miracles. I have felt angels. I have known that my Heavenly Father was carrying me. None of that would have been experienced if life was easy. The future of this life may be unknown, but my faith is not. If I choose to not have faith then I choose to only walk in darkness. Because without faith, darkness is all that is left."[10]

Her unshakable testimony of faith in the Lord Jesus Christ—in her words and in her actions—was an inspiration for others. Even though her body was *weak,* she lifted others to be *stronger.*

I think of countless other members of the Church, warriors like this sister, who walk each day in faith, striving to be true and undaunted disciples of our Savior, Jesus Christ. They learn of Christ. They preach of Christ. They strive to emulate Him. Whether the days of their lives face steady or unstable ground, their spiritual foundation is strong and immovable.

These are the devoted souls who understand the profound meaning of the lyrics "How firm a foundation, ye Saints of the Lord" and "who unto the Savior for refuge have fled."[11] I am grateful beyond measure to walk among those who have prepared a spiritual foundation worthy of the name of *Saints* and who are strong and secure enough to withstand the many tumults of life.

I don't think we can overstate the importance of such a firm foundation in our personal lives. Even at an early age, our Primary children are taught as they sing of this very truth:

> *The wise man built his house upon the rock,*
> *And the rains came tumbling down. . . .*
> *The rains came down, and the floods came up,*
> *And the house on the rock stood still.*[12]

Scripture reinforces this foundational doctrine. The Savior taught the people of the Americas:

"And if ye shall always do these things blessed are ye, for ye are *built upon my rock.*

"But whoso among you shall do more or less than these are *not built upon my rock,* but are built upon a sandy foundation; and when the rain descends, and the floods come, and the winds blow, and beat upon them, they shall fall."[13]

It is the sincere hope of Church leaders that the significant renovations to the Salt Lake Temple will contribute to the fulfillment of Brigham Young's desire to see "the temple built in a manner that it will endure through the millennium." During the coming years, may we allow these improvements made to the Salt Lake Temple to move and inspire us, as individuals and families, so that we too—metaphorically—will "be built in a manner that will endure through the millennium."

We will do so as we fulfill the charge of the Apostle Paul to "[lay] up in store for [ourselves] *a good foundation against the time to come,* that [we] may lay hold on eternal life."[14] It is my ardent prayer that our spiritual foundation will be sure and steadfast, that our testimony of the Atonement of Jesus Christ and of His role as our Savior and Redeemer will become for us our own chief cornerstone, of whom I testify in His name, even Jesus Christ, amen.

Notes

1. William Clayton journal, July 26, 1847, Church History Library, Salt Lake City.
2. See "At the Tabernacle, Presidents Woodruff and Smith Address the Saints Yesterday Afternoon," *Deseret Evening News,* Aug. 30, 1897, 5; "Pioneers' Day," *Deseret Evening News,* July 26, 1880, 2; Wilford Woodruff journal, July 28, 1847, Church History Library, Salt Lake City.
3. "Minutes of the General Conference of the Church of Jesus Christ of Latter-day Saints, held at Great Salt Lake City, State of Deseret, April 6, 1851," *Deseret News,* Apr. 19, 1851, 241.
4. See "The Temple," *Deseret News,* Feb. 19, 1853, 130; "Minutes of the General Conference," *Deseret News,* Apr. 16, 1853, 146; "Minutes of the General Conference," *Deseret News,* Apr. 30, 1853, 150.
5. "Address by President Brigham Young," *Millennial Star,* Apr. 22, 1854, 241.
6. "Remarks by President Brigham Young," *Deseret News,* Oct. 14, 1863, 97.
7. Presiding Bishopric presentation on the Salt Lake Temple to the First Presidency, Oct. 2015.
8. See Russell M. Nelson, "Closing Remarks," *Ensign* or *Liahona,* Nov. 2019, 121.
9. Ephesians 2:20–21.
10. Social media post by Kim Olsen White.
11. "How Firm a Foundation," *Hymns,* no. 85.
12. "The Wise Man and the Foolish Man," *Children's Songbook,* 281; emphasis in original was removed in this instance.
13. 3 Nephi 18:12–13; emphasis added.
14. 1 Timothy 6:19; emphasis added.

HOSANNA AND HALLELUJAH—THE LIVING JESUS CHRIST: THE HEART OF RESTORATION AND EASTER

ELDER GERRIT W. GONG
Of the Quorum of the Twelve Apostles

Dear brothers and sisters: with hosanna and hallelujah, we celebrate the living Jesus Christ at this season of continuing Restoration and Easter. With perfect love, our Savior assures us: "In me ye might have peace. In the world ye shall have tribulation: but be of good cheer; I have overcome the world."[1]

Some years ago, as Sister Gong and I met a lovely family, their young daughter, Ivy, shyly brought out her violin case. She lifted out the violin bow, tightened and put rosin on it. Then she put the bow back in the case, curtsied, and sat down. A new beginner, she had just shared all she knew about the violin. Now, years later, Ivy plays the violin beautifully.

In this mortal period, we are all a little like Ivy and her violin. We begin at the beginning. With practice and persistence, we grow and improve. With the passage of time, moral agency and mortal experiences help us become more like our Savior as we labor with Him in His vineyard[2] and follow His covenant path.

Anniversaries, including this bicentennial, highlight patterns of restoration.[3] In celebrating the ongoing Restoration of the gospel of Jesus Christ, we also prepare for Easter. In both, we rejoice in the return of Jesus Christ. He lives—not only then, but now; not just for some, but for all. He came and comes to heal the brokenhearted, deliver the captives, recover sight to the blind, and set at liberty those who are bruised.[4] That's each of us. His redeeming promises apply, no matter our past, our present, or concerns for our future.

Tomorrow is Palm Sunday. Traditionally, palms are a sacred symbol to express joy in our Lord, as in *Christ's Triumphal Entry into Jerusalem*, where "much people . . . took branches of palm trees, and went forth to meet him."[5] (You may be interested to know the original of this Harry Anderson painting hangs in President

Russell M. Nelson's office, just behind his desk.) In the book of Revelation, those who praise God and the Lamb do so "clothed with white robes, and palms in their hands."[6] Along with "robes of righteousness" and "crowns of glory," palms are included in the Kirtland Temple dedicatory prayer.[7]

Of course, the significance of Palm Sunday goes beyond crowds greeting Jesus with palms. On Palm Sunday, Jesus entered Jerusalem in ways the faithful recognized as fulfillment of prophecy. As Zechariah[8] and the Psalmist prophetically foretold, our Lord entered Jerusalem riding a colt as multitudes knowingly cried, "Hosanna in the highest."[9] Hosanna means "save now."[10] Then, as now, we rejoice, "Blessed be he that cometh in the name of the Lord."[11]

A week following Palm Sunday is Easter Sunday. President Russell M. Nelson teaches that Jesus Christ "came to pay a debt He didn't owe because we owed a debt we couldn't pay."[12] Indeed, through the Atonement of Christ, all God's children "may be saved, by obedience to the laws and ordinances of the Gospel."[13] At Easter, we sing hallelujah. Hallelujah means "praise ye the Lord Jehovah."[14] The "Hallelujah Chorus" in Handel's *Messiah* is a beloved Easter declaration that He is "King of Kings, and Lord of Lords."[15]

The sacred events between Palm Sunday and Easter Sunday are the story of hosanna and hallelujah. Hosanna is our plea for God to save. Hallelujah expresses our praise to the Lord for the hope of salvation and exaltation. In hosanna and hallelujah we recognize the living Jesus Christ as the heart of Easter and latter-day restoration.

Latter-day restoration begins with theophany—the literal appearance of God the Father and His Son, Jesus Christ, to the young prophet Joseph Smith. Said the Prophet Joseph, "Could you gaze into heaven five minutes, you would know more than you would by reading all that ever was written on the subject."[16] Because the heavens are again open, we know and "believe in God, the Eternal Father, and in His Son, Jesus Christ, and in the Holy Ghost"[17]—the divine Godhead.

On Easter Sunday, April 3, 1836, in the early days of the Restoration, the living Jesus Christ appeared after the Kirtland

Temple was dedicated. Those who saw Him there testified of Him in complementary contrasts of fire and water: "His eyes were as a flame of *fire;* the hair of his head was white like the *pure snow;* his countenance shone above the *brightness of the sun;* and his voice was as the sound of the *rushing of great waters,* even the voice of Jehovah."[18]

On that occasion, our Savior declared, "I am the first and the last; I am he who liveth, I am he who was slain; I am your advocate with the Father."[19] Again, complementary contrasts—first and last, living and slain. He is Alpha and Omega, the beginning and the end,[20] the author and finisher of our faith.[21]

Following the appearance of Jesus Christ, Moses, Elias, and Elijah also came. By divine direction, these great prophets of old restored priesthood keys and authority. Thus, "the keys of this dispensation are committed"[22] within His restored Church to bless all God's children.

The coming of Elijah in the Kirtland Temple also fulfilled Malachi's Old Testament prophecy that Elijah would return "before the coming of the great and dreadful day of the Lord."[23] In doing so, Elijah's appearance coincided, though not by coincidence, with the Jewish Passover season, which tradition reverently anticipates Elijah's return.

Many devout Jewish families set a place for Elijah at their Passover table. Many fill a cup to the brim to invite and welcome him. And some, during the traditional Passover Seder, send a child to the door, sometimes left partly open, to see if Elijah is outside waiting to be invited in.[24]

In fulfillment of prophecy and as part of the promised restoration of all things,[25] Elijah did come as promised, at Easter and the onset of Passover. He brought the sealing authority to bind families on earth and in heaven. As Moroni taught the Prophet Joseph, Elijah "shall plant in the hearts of the children the promises made to the fathers, and the hearts of the children shall turn to their fathers. If it were not so," Moroni continued, "the whole earth would be utterly wasted at [the Lord's] coming."[26] The spirit of Elijah, a manifestation of the Holy Ghost, draws us to our generations—past, present, and future—in our genealogies, histories, and temple service.

Let us also briefly recall what Passover signifies. Passover remembers the deliverance of the children of Israel from 400 years of bondage. The book of Exodus relates how this deliverance came after plagues of frogs, lice, flies, the death of cattle, boils, blains, hail and fire, locusts, and thick darkness. The final plague threatened the death of the firstborn in the land but not in the house of Israel if—if those households put the blood of an unblemished firstling lamb on the lintels of their doors.[27]

The angel of death passed by the houses marked with the symbolic blood of the lamb.[28] That passing by, or pass over, represents Jesus Christ ultimately overcoming death. Indeed, the atoning blood of the Lamb of God gives our Good Shepherd power to gather His people in all places and circumstances into the safety of His fold on both sides of the veil.

Significantly, the Book of Mormon describes the "power and resurrection of Christ"[29]—the essence of Easter—in terms of two restorations.

First, resurrection includes physical restoration of our "proper and perfect frame"; "every limb and joint," "even a hair of the head shall not be lost."[30] This promise gives hope to those who have lost limbs; those who have lost ability to see, hear, or walk; or those thought lost to relentless disease, mental illness, or other diminished capacity. He finds us. He makes us whole.

A second promise of Easter and our Lord's Atonement is that, spiritually, "all things shall be restored to their proper order."[31] This spiritual restoration reflects our works and desires. Like bread upon the water,[32] it restores "that which is good," "righteous," "just," and "merciful."[33] No wonder the prophet Alma uses the word *restore* 22 times[34] as he urges us to "deal justly, judge righteously, and do good continually."[35]

Because "God himself atoneth for the sins of the world,"[36] the Lord's Atonement can make whole not only what was but also what can be. Because He knows ours pains, afflictions, sicknesses, our "temptations of every kind,"[37] He can, with mercy, succor us according to our infirmities.[38] Because God is "a perfect, just God, and a merciful God also," the plan of mercy can "appease the demands of justice."[39] We repent and do all we can. He encircles us eternally "in the arms of his love."[40]

Today we celebrate restoration and resurrection. With you, I rejoice in the ongoing Restoration of the fulness of the gospel of Jesus Christ. As began 200 years ago this spring, light and revelation continue to come forth through the Lord's living prophet and His Church called in His name—The Church of Jesus Christ of Latter-day Saints—and through personal revelation and inspiration by the supernal gift of the Holy Ghost.

With you, at this Easter season, I testify of God, our Eternal Father, and His Beloved Son, the living Jesus Christ. Mortal men were cruelly crucified and later resurrected. But only the living Jesus Christ in His perfect resurrected form still bears the marks of crucifixion in His hands, feet, and side. Only He can say, "I have graven thee upon the palms of my hands."[41] Only He can say: "I am he who was lifted up. I am Jesus that was crucified. I am the Son of God."[42]

Like little Ivy and her violin, we are in some ways still beginning. Truly, "eye hath not seen, nor ear heard, neither have entered into the heart of man, the things which God hath prepared for them that love him."[43] In these times, we can learn much of God's goodness and our divine potential for God's love to grow in us as we seek Him and reach out to each other. In new ways and new places, we can do and become, line upon line, kindness upon kindness, individually and together.

Dear brothers and sisters everywhere, as we meet and learn together, your faith and goodness fill me with a sense of gospel adventure and gratitude. Your testimony and gospel journey enrich my testimony and gospel journey. Your concerns and joys, your love for the household of God and community of Saints, and your lived understanding of restored truth and light increase my fulness of the restored gospel, with the living Jesus Christ at its heart. Together we trust, "thru cloud and sunshine, Lord, abide with me."[44] Unitedly we know, amidst our loads and cares, we can count our many blessings.[45] In the daily details and small and simple things, we can see great things brought to pass in our lives.[46]

"And it shall come to pass that the righteous shall be gathered out from among all nations, and shall come to Zion, singing with songs of everlasting joy."[47] At this season of hosanna and hallelujah, sing hallelujah—for He shall reign forever and ever! Shout hosanna, to God and the Lamb! In the sacred and holy name of Jesus Christ, amen.

Notes

1. John 16:33.
2. See Jacob 5.
3. As scripturally prophesied, human history manifests periods or cycles of spiritual decline we call apostasy or falling away, and periods of renewed light we call spiritual restoration; see, for example, 2 Thessalonians 2:3.
4. See Luke 4:18.
5. John 12:12–13; see also Matthew 21:8–9; Mark 11:8–10.
6. Revelation 7:9.
7. See Doctrine and Covenants 109:76.
8. See Zechariah 9:9.
9. Matthew 21:9.
10. See Bible Dictionary, "Hosanna." From Old Testament times, the waving of palm branches accompanied the chanting of "Save now, I beseech thee, O Lord." Psalm 118:25 is the full expression of the traditional chiastic Messianic plea: "Save now, I beseech thee, O Lord: O Lord, I beseech thee, send now prosperity."
11. Psalm 118:26
12. Russell M. Nelson, in *Handel's Messiah: Debtor's Prison* (video), ChurchofJesusChrist.org/media-library.
13. Articles of Faith 1:3.
14. See Bible Dictionary, "Hallelujah."
15. George Frideric Handel, *Messiah,* ed. T. Tertius Noble (1912), viii; see also Revelation 17:14.
16. *Teachings of Presidents of the Church: Joseph Smith* (2007), 419.
17. Articles of Faith 1:1.
18. Doctrine and Covenants 110:3; emphasis added.
19. Doctrine and Covenants 110:4.
20. See Revelation 1:8; 3 Nephi 9:18; Doctrine and Covenants 19:1; 38:1; 45:7.
21. See Hebrews 12:2; Moroni 6:4.
22. Doctrine and Covenants 110:16.
23. Malachi 4:5.
24. See Stephen D. Ricks, "The Appearance of Elijah and Moses in the Kirtland Temple and the Jewish Passover," *BYU Studies,* vol. 23, no. 4 (1986), 483–86, byustudies.byu.edu.
25. See Doctrine and Covenants 86:10; see also Acts 3:19–21.
26. Joseph Smith—History 1:39; in recent years, many have thought significant the specific possessive "their."
27. See Exodus 7–12.
28. See Exodus 12:23.

29. Alma 41:2.
30. Alma 40:23.
31. Alma 41:4.
32. See Ecclesiastes 11:1.
33. Alma 41:13.
34. The words *restore, restored, restoration,* or other variants appear 22 times in Alma 40:22–24 and in Alma 41, emphasizing both physical and spiritual restoration.
35. Alma 41:14.
36. Alma 42:15.
37. Alma 7:11.
38. See Alma 7:12.
39. Alma 42:15.
40. 2 Nephi 1:15.
41. Isaiah 49:16; 1 Nephi 21:16.
42. Doctrine and Covenants 45:52.
43. 1 Corinthians 2:9.
44. "Abide with Me!" *Hymns,* no. 166.
45. See "Count Your Blessings," *Hymns,* no. 241.
46. See Alma 37:6.
47. Doctrine and Covenants 45:71.

HOW THE PRIESTHOOD BLESSES YOUTH

LAUDY RUTH KAOUK
Member of the Slate Canyon 14th Ward (Spanish), Provo Utah Stake

I am grateful to be here. When I first found out I would have the opportunity to speak to you today, I felt very excited but at the same time very humbled. I have spent a lot of time thinking about what I could share, and I hope the Spirit speaks to you directly through my message.

In the Book of Mormon, Lehi gives a blessing to each of his sons before he passes away that helps them to see their strengths and eternal potential. I am the youngest of eight children, and this past year I have been the only child at home for the first time. Not having my siblings close by and not always having someone to talk to has been hard for me. There have been nights when I have felt very lonely. I'm grateful for my parents, who have tried their best to help me. An example of this is when my dad offered to give me a priesthood blessing of comfort during a particularly challenging time. After his blessing, things didn't change right away, but I was able to feel peace and love from my Heavenly Father and from my dad. I feel blessed to have a worthy father who can provide priesthood blessings whenever I need them and who helps me to see my strengths and eternal potential, just as Lehi did when he blessed his children.

Regardless of your circumstances, you can always have access to priesthood blessings. Through family members, friends, ministering brothers, priesthood leaders, and a Heavenly Father who will never fail you, you can receive the blessings of the priesthood. Elder Neil L. Andersen said: "The blessings of the priesthood are infinitely greater than the one who is asked to administer the gift. . . . As we are worthy, the ordinances of the priesthood enrich our lives."[1]

Don't hesitate to ask for a blessing when you need extra guidance. It is in our difficult moments that we need the Spirit to help us the most. No one is perfect, and we all experience hardships. Some of us might suffer with anxiety, depression, addiction, or feelings that we are not enough. Priesthood blessings can help us overcome these challenges and receive peace as we move forward into the future. I hope that we strive to live worthy of receiving these blessings.

Another way the priesthood blesses us is through patriarchal blessings. I have learned to turn to my patriarchal blessing whenever I feel sad or lonely. My blessing helps me to see my potential and the specific plan God has for me. It comforts me and helps me to see beyond my earthly perspective. It reminds me of my gifts and of the blessings I will receive if I live worthily. It also helps me to remember and feel at peace that God will provide answers and open doors for me at exactly the right moment when I need it most.

Patriarchal blessings help prepare us to return to live with our Heavenly Father. I know patriarchal blessings come from God and can help us turn our weaknesses into strengths. These are not messages from fortune-tellers; these blessings tell us what we need to hear. They are like a Liahona for each one of us. When we put God first and have faith in Him, He will lead us through our own wilderness.

Just like God blessed Joseph Smith with the priesthood so that the blessings of the gospel could be restored, we can receive the blessings of the gospel in our lives through the priesthood. Each week we are given the privilege and opportunity of taking the sacrament. Through this priesthood ordinance, we can have the Spirit to always be with us, which can cleanse and purify us. If you feel the need to eliminate something from your life, reach out to a trusted leader who can help you get on the right path. Your leaders can help you to access the full power of the Atonement of Jesus Christ.

Thanks to the priesthood, we can also receive the blessings of ordinances of the temple. Ever since I've been able to enter the temple, I have made it a goal and priority to attend regularly. By taking the time and making the sacrifices necessary to be closer to my Heavenly Father in His holy house, I have been blessed with receiving revelation and promptings that have really helped me throughout my life.

Through the priesthood, we can be lifted. The priesthood brings light into our world. Elder Robert D. Hales said: "Without the power of the priesthood, 'the whole earth would be utterly wasted' (see D&C 2:1–3). There would be no light, no hope—only darkness."[2]

God is cheering for us. He wants us to return to Him. He knows us personally. He knows you. He loves us. He is always aware of us and blesses us even when we feel we don't deserve it. He knows what we need and when we need it.

"Ask, and it shall be given you; seek, and ye shall find; knock, and it shall be opened unto you:

"For every one that asketh receiveth; and he that seeketh findeth; and to him that knocketh it shall be opened" (Matthew 7:7–8).

If you don't already have a testimony about the priesthood, I encourage you to pray and ask to know for yourself of its power, then read the scriptures to hear God's words. I know that if we make an effort to experience the power of God's priesthood in our lives, we will be blessed. In the name of Jesus Christ, amen.

Notes
1. Neil L. Andersen, "Power in the Priesthood," *Ensign* or *Liahona,* Nov. 2013, 92.
2. Robert D. Hales, "Blessings of the Priesthood," *Ensign,* Nov. 1995, 32.

HOW THE PRIESTHOOD BLESSES YOUTH

ENZO SERGE PETELO
Member of the Meadow Wood Ward, Provo Utah Edgemont Stake

Brothers and sisters, I am truly grateful to speak to you on this historic evening about the sacred gift of the priesthood and the marvelous power it has to bless the youth in this dispensation. I pray that despite my imperfections, the Spirit will assist me in teaching truth.

The First Presidency has reminded holders of the Aaronic Priesthood that "you live in a day of great opportunities and challenges—a day in which the priesthood has been restored. You have the authority to administer the ordinances of the Aaronic Priesthood. As you prayerfully and worthily exercise that authority, you will greatly bless the lives of those around you."[1] As the young men of the Church, we are also reminded that we are "beloved [sons] of God, and He has a work for [us] to do,"[2] and we assist in His work "to bring to pass the immortality and eternal life of man" (Moses 1:39).

The priesthood is the authority to administer the ordinances and covenants of the Savior's gospel to those who are worthy to receive them. Through these priesthood ordinances and sacred covenants come the full blessings of the Savior's Atonement, which helps us achieve our divine destiny.

Joseph Smith was a young man who was called of God to restore the gospel of Jesus Christ and, for that purpose, was given the priesthood, which he used to bless all mankind. Doctrine and Covenants 135 cites many of the blessings Joseph has given the youth of this dispensation. We read: "Joseph Smith . . . has done more, save Jesus only, for the salvation of men in this world, than any other man that ever lived in it. . . . He has brought forth the Book of Mormon . . . ; has sent the fulness of the everlasting gospel . . . to the four quarters of the earth; has brought forth the revelations and commandments which compose [the] Doctrine and Covenants . . . ; gathered many thousands of the Latter-day Saints, . . . and left a fame and name that cannot be slain" (Doctrine and Covenants 135:3).

To effectively serve like Joseph did, we must worthily qualify to use the Lord's priesthood power. While translating the Book of Mormon, Joseph and Oliver Cowdery wanted to be baptized, but they lacked the proper authority. On May 15, 1829, they knelt in prayer and were visited by John the Baptist, who gave them the keys and authority of the Aaronic Priesthood, saying, "Upon you my fellow servants, in the name of Messiah I confer the Priesthood of Aaron, which holds the keys of the ministering of angels, and of the gospel of repentance, and of baptism by immersion for the remission of sins" (Doctrine and Covenants 13:1).

We are given the opportunity to minister like angels, to preach the gospel on all the continents of the earth, and to help souls come unto Christ. This service places us in joint labor with John the Baptist, Moroni, Joseph Smith, President Russell M. Nelson, and other diligent servants of the Lord.

Our service in and with His priesthood brings together those who are dedicated to following and living the Lord's teachings with exactness, which I personally know can be difficult as we face the challenges of youth. But uniting with these fellow servants of the Lord in accomplishing His work will help to strengthen us against the adversary's temptations and deceptions. You can be a beacon of light to all those who are unsure of themselves. The light within you will shine so bright that everyone you interact with will be blessed by just being in your company. It may be hard at times to acknowledge the presence of our spiritual companions, but I am grateful to know that I am a member of a faithful priesthood quorum with whom I can work to grow closer to Christ.

Along with our friends and family, the Holy Ghost is one of our most loyal and reliable companions. But in order to invite His constant companionship, we must place ourselves in situations and places where He will want to be present. This can begin in our own homes as we work to make them holy places by participating in daily scripture study and prayer as a family and, more important, as we personally study the scriptures and pray on our own.

Earlier this year, I was provided with an exciting yet humbling opportunity to help my little sister, Oceane, progress on the covenant path by accepting the invitation to be baptized and fulfill one of the prescribed requirements to enter the celestial kingdom. She postponed her baptism one month, until I was ordained a priest, to give me the privilege to perform the ordinance, while our other sisters were also privileged to work under priesthood assignment and stand as witnesses. As we stood on opposite sides of the font and prepared to enter the water, I noticed her excitement, as it matched mine. And I felt united with her, seeing that she was making the right decision. This opportunity to exercise the priesthood required me to be more careful and less casual in my gospel living. In order to prepare, I went to the temple every day that week, supported by my mom, grandma, and sister, to perform baptisms for the dead.

This experience taught me a lot about the priesthood and how I could exercise it worthily. I know that all priesthood holders can feel the same things I felt if we follow Nephi's example to "go and do" (see 1 Nephi 3:7). We cannot sit idly and expect the Lord to use us in His great work. We must not wait for those who need our aid to seek us out; it is our duty as priesthood holders to exemplify and stand as witnesses of God. If we are making decisions that inhibit us from our eternal progression, we must change now. Satan will try his hardest to keep us in a carnal state of seeking simple pleasures. But I know that if we put in the effort, find those who will support us, and repent each day, the resulting blessings will be incredible and our lives will be forever changed as we press forward on the covenant path.

I know that this is the true Church of Jesus Christ, who is our Savior and has delegated the keys of the priesthood to His Apostles, who use it to guide us, especially in these challenging days, and to prepare the world for His return.

I know that Joseph Smith was the prophet of the Restoration and that President Nelson is our living prophet today. I invite all of us to study the lives of these great priesthood holders and seek to improve ourselves daily so we can be ready to meet our Maker. In the name of Jesus Christ, amen.

Notes

1. The First Presidency, in *Fulfilling My Duty to God* (booklet, 2010), 5.
2. Aaronic Priesthood quorum theme, in *General Handbook: Serving in The Church of Jesus Christ of Latter-day Saints,* 10.1.2, ChurchofJesusChrist.org.

UNITED IN ACCOMPLISHING GOD'S WORK

JEAN B. BINGHAM
Relief Society General President

Dear wonderful sisters and brothers, it is a delight to be with you. Wherever you are listening, I extend hugs to my sisters and heartfelt handshakes to my brothers. We are united in the work of the Lord.

When we think of Adam and Eve, often our first thought is of their idyllic life in the Garden of Eden. I imagine that the weather was always perfect—not too hot and not too cold—and that abundant, delicious fruits and vegetables grew within reach so they could eat whenever they liked. Since this was a new world for them, there was much to discover, so every day was interesting as they interacted with the animal life and explored their beautiful surroundings. They also were given commandments to obey and had different ways of approaching those instructions, which caused some initial anxiety and confusion.[1] But as they made decisions that changed their lives forever, they learned to work together and became united in accomplishing the purposes God had for them—and for all of His children.

Now picture this same couple in mortality. They had to labor for their food, some of the animals considered *them* food, and there were difficult challenges that could be overcome only as they counseled and prayed together. I imagine there were at least a few times they had differing opinions about how to approach those challenges. However, through the Fall, they had learned that it was essential to act in unity and love. In the tutoring they received from divine sources, they were taught the plan of salvation and the principles of the gospel of Jesus Christ that make the plan operable. Because they understood that their earthly purpose and eternal goal were identical, they found satisfaction and success in learning to labor in love and righteousness together.

As children were born to them, Adam and Eve taught their

family what they had learned from heavenly messengers. They were focused on helping their children also understand and embrace those principles that would make them happy in this life, as well as prepared to return to their heavenly parents after having increased their abilities and proved their obedience to God. In the process, Adam and Eve learned to appreciate their differing strengths and supported one another in their eternally significant work.[2]

As centuries and then millennia came and went, the clarity of men's and women's inspired and interdependent contributions became clouded with misinformation and misunderstandings. During the time between that marvelous beginning in the Garden of Eden and now, the adversary has been quite successful in his goal to divide men and women in his attempts to conquer our souls. Lucifer knows that if he can damage the unity men and women feel, if he can confuse us about our divine worth and covenant responsibilities, he will succeed in destroying families, which are the essential units of eternity.

Satan incites comparison as a tool to create feelings of being superior or inferior, hiding the eternal truth that men's and women's innate differences are God given and equally valued. He has attempted to demean women's contributions both to the family and in civil society, thereby decreasing their uplifting influence for good. His goal has been to foster a power struggle rather than a celebration of the unique contributions of men and women that complement one another and contribute to unity.

So, over the years and around the globe, a full understanding of the divinely interdependent and yet differing contributions and responsibilities of women and men largely disappeared. Females in many societies became subservient to males rather than side-by-side partners, their activities limited to a narrow scope. Spiritual progress slowed to a trickle during those dark times; indeed, little spiritual light could penetrate minds and hearts steeped in traditions of dominance.

And then the light of the restored gospel shone "above the brightness of the sun"[3] when God the Father and His Son, Jesus

Christ, appeared to the boy Joseph Smith early in the spring of 1820 in that hallowed woodland in upstate New York. That event began a modern outpouring of revelation from heaven. One of the first elements of Christ's original Church to be restored was the authority of the priesthood of God. As the Restoration continued to unfold, men and women began to realize anew the importance and potential of working as partners, authorized and directed in this sacred labor by Him.

In 1842, when the women of the fledgling Church wanted to form an official group to help in the work, President Joseph Smith felt inspired to organize them "under the priesthood after the pattern of the priesthood."[4] He said, "I now turn the key to you in the name of God . . . —this is the beginning of better days."[5] And since that key was turned, educational, political, and economic opportunities for women have begun to gradually expand throughout the world.[6]

This new Church organization for women, named the Relief Society, was unlike other women's societies of the day because it was established by a prophet who acted with priesthood authority to give women authority, sacred responsibilities, and official positions within the structure of the Church, not apart from it.[7]

From the Prophet Joseph Smith's day to ours, the ongoing restoration of all things has brought enlightenment on the necessity of the authority and power of the priesthood in helping both men and women accomplish their divinely appointed responsibilities. Recently we have been taught that women who are set apart under the direction of one holding priesthood keys operate with *priesthood authority* in their callings.[8]

In October 2019, President Russell M. Nelson taught that women who are endowed in the temple have *priesthood power* in their lives and in their homes as they keep those sacred covenants they made with God.[9] He explained that "the heavens are just as open to *women* who are endowed with God's power flowing from their priesthood covenants as they are to men who bear the priesthood." And he encouraged every sister to "draw liberally upon the Savior's power to help your family and others you love."[10]

So what does that mean for you and me? How does understanding priesthood authority and power change our lives? One of the keys is to understand that when women and men work together, we accomplish a great deal more than we do working separately.[11] Our roles are complementary rather than competitive. Although women are not ordained to a priesthood office, as noted previously women are blessed with priesthood power as they keep their covenants, and they operate with priesthood authority when they are set apart to a calling.

On a lovely August day, I was privileged to sit down with President Russell M. Nelson in the reconstructed home of Joseph and Emma Smith in Harmony, Pennsylvania, near where the Aaronic Priesthood was restored in these latter days. In our conversation, President Nelson talked about the important role women played in the Restoration.

> PRESIDENT NELSON: "One of the most important aspects that I am reminded of when I come to this restoration of the priesthood site is the important role that women played in the Restoration.
>
> "When Joseph first started to translate the Book of Mormon, who did the writing? Well, he did a little, but not much. Emma stepped in.
>
> "And then I think of how Joseph went into the woods to pray near their home in Palmyra, New York. Where did he go? He went to the Sacred Grove. Why did he go there? Because that's where Mother went when she wanted to pray.
>
> "Those are just two of the women who had key roles in the restoration of the priesthood and in the Restoration of the Church. No doubt, we could say our wives are just as important today as they were then. Of course they are."

Like Emma and Lucy and Joseph, we are most effective when we are willing to learn from one another and are united in our goal to become disciples of Jesus Christ and help others along that path.

We are taught that "priesthood blesses the lives of God's children in innumerable ways. . . . In [Church] callings, temple ordinances, family relationships, and quiet, individual ministry, Latter-day Saint women and men go forward with priesthood power and authority. This interdependence of men and women in accomplishing God's work through His power is central to the gospel of Jesus Christ restored through the Prophet Joseph Smith."[12]

Unity is essential to the divine work we are privileged and called to do, but it doesn't just happen. It takes effort and time to really counsel together—to listen to one another, understand others' viewpoints, and share experiences—but the process results in more inspired decisions. Whether at home or in our Church responsibilities, the most effective way to fulfill our divine potential is to work together, blessed by the power and authority of the priesthood in our differing yet complementary roles.

What does that partnership look like in the lives of covenant women today? Let me share an example.

Alison and John had a partnership that was unique. They rode a tandem bicycle in races short and long. To successfully compete on that vehicle, the two riders must be in harmony. They have to lean in the same direction at the right time. One cannot dominate the other, but they must communicate clearly and each do his or her part. The captain, in front, has control over when to brake and when to stand. The stoker, in the back, needs to pay attention to what is going on and be ready to give extra power if they lag behind a little or to ease up if they get too close to other cyclists. They must support one another to make progress and achieve their goal.

Alison explained: "For the first little while, the person in the captain position would say 'Stand' when we needed to stand and 'Braking' when we needed to stop pedaling. After a while, the person who was the stoker learned to tell when the captain was about to stand or brake, and no words needed to be said. We learned to be in tune to how each other was doing and could tell when one was struggling and [then] the other tried to pick up the slack. It's really all about trust and working together."[13]

John and Alison were united not only as they pedaled their bicycle, but they were united in their marriage as well. Each desired the happiness of the other more than his or her own; each looked for the good in one another and worked to overcome the not-so-great in him or herself. They took turns leading and took turns giving more when one partner was struggling. Each valued the other's contributions and found better answers to their challenges as they combined their talents and resources. They are truly bound to one another through Christlike love.

Becoming more in tune with the divine pattern of working together in unity is critical in this day of "me first" messages that surround us. Women do possess distinctive, divine gifts[14] and are given unique responsibilities, but those are not more—or less—important than men's gifts and responsibilities. *All* are designed and needed to bring about Heavenly Father's divine plan to give each of His children the best opportunity to fulfill his or her divine potential.

Today, "we need women who have the courage and vision of our Mother Eve"[15] to unite with their brethren in bringing souls unto Christ.[16] Men need to become true partners rather than assume they are solely responsible or act as "pretend" partners while women carry out much of the work. Women need to be willing to "step forward [and] take [their] rightful and needful place"[17] as partners rather than thinking they need to do it all by themselves or wait to be told what to do.[18]

Seeing women as vital participants is not about creating parity but about understanding doctrinal truth. Rather than establishing a program to bring that about, we can actively work to value women as God does: as essential partners in the work of salvation and exaltation.

Are we ready? Will we strive to overcome cultural bias and instead embrace divine patterns and practices based on foundational doctrine? President Russell M. Nelson invites us to "walk arm in arm in this sacred work . . . [to] help prepare the world for the Second Coming of the Lord."[19] As we do, we will learn to value each individual's contributions and increase the effectiveness with which we fulfill our divine roles. We will feel greater joy than we have ever experienced.

May each of us choose to become united in the Lord's inspired way to help His work go forward. In the name of our beloved Savior, Jesus Christ, amen.

Notes

1. See Genesis 3:1–18; Moses 4:1–19.
2. See Moses 5:1–12. These verses teach of Adam and Eve's true partnership: they had children together (verse 2); they labored together in providing for themselves and their family (verse 1); they prayed together (verse 4); they obeyed the commandments of God and offered sacrifices together (verse 5); they learned (verses 4, 6–11) and taught the gospel of Jesus Christ to their children together (verse 12).
3. Joseph Smith—History 1:16.
4. Joseph Smith, in Sarah M. Kimball, "Auto-Biography," *Woman's Exponent,* Sept. 1, 1883, 51; see also *Teachings of Presidents of the Church: Joseph Smith* (2007), 451.
5. Joseph Smith, in "Nauvoo Relief Society Minute Book," 40, josephsmithpapers.org.
6. See George Albert Smith, "Address to the Members of the Relief Society," *Relief Society Magazine,* Dec. 1945, 717.
7. See John Taylor, in Nauvoo Relief Society Minutes, Mar. 17, 1842, available at churchhistorianspress.org. According to Eliza R. Snow, Joseph Smith also taught that women had been formally organized in previous dispensations (see Eliza R. Snow, "Female Relief Society," *Deseret News,* Apr. 22, 1868, 1; *Daughters in My Kingdom: The History and Work of Relief Society* [2011], 1–7).
8. See Dallin H. Oaks, "The Keys and Authority of the Priesthood," *Ensign* or *Liahona,* May 2014, 49–52.
9. See Russell M. Nelson, "Spiritual Treasures," *Ensign* or *Liahona,* Nov. 2019, 78, 79.
10. Russell M. Nelson, "Spiritual Treasures," 77.
11. "But the restored gospel teaches the eternal idea that husbands and wives are *interdependent* with each other. They are equal. They are partners" (Bruce R. and Marie K. Hafen, "Crossing Thresholds and Becoming Equal Partners," *Ensign,* Aug. 2007, 26; *Liahona,* Aug. 2007, 28).
12. Gospel Topics, "Joseph Smith's Teachings about Priesthood, Temple, and Women," topics.ChurchofJesusChrist.org.
13. Personal correspondence.
14. See Russell M. Nelson, "A Plea to My Sisters," *Ensign* or *Liahona,* Nov. 2015, 95–97.
15. Russell M. Nelson, "A Plea to My Sisters," 97.
16. See *General Handbook: Serving in The Church of Jesus Christ of Latter-day Saints,* 1.4, ChurchofJesusChrist.org.
17. Russell M. Nelson, "A Plea to My Sisters," 97.
18. "My dear sisters, whatever your calling, whatever your circumstances, we need your impressions, your insights, and your inspiration. We need you to speak up and speak out in ward and stake councils. We need each married sister to speak as 'a *contributing* and *full* partner' as you unite with your husband in governing your family. Married or single, you sisters possess distinctive capabilities and special intuition you have received as gifts from God. We brethren cannot duplicate your unique influence. . . .

    ". . . We need your strength!" (Russell M. Nelson, "A Plea to My Sisters," 97).
19. Russell M. Nelson, "A Plea to My Sisters," 97.

HE GOES BEFORE US

PRESIDENT HENRY B. EYRING
Second Counselor in the First Presidency

My beloved brothers and sisters, I am grateful to be with you in this general conference of The Church of Jesus Christ of Latter-day Saints. In his invitation to reflect on the way the Lord's Restoration of His Church in this last dispensation has blessed us and our loved ones, President Russell M. Nelson promised that our experience would be not only memorable but unforgettable.

My experience has been memorable, as I am sure yours has been. Whether it will be unforgettable depends on each one of us. That matters to me because the experience of preparing for this conference has changed me in a way that I want to last. Let me explain.

My preparation took me to the record of an event in the Restoration. I had read about that event many times, but it had always been to me a report of an important meeting that involved Joseph Smith, the prophet of the Restoration. But this time I saw in the account how the Lord leads us, His disciples, in His Church. I saw what it means for us mortals to be led by the Savior of the world, the Creator—who knows all things, past, present, and future. He teaches us step by step and guides us, never forcing.

The meeting I'm describing was a pivotal moment in the Restoration. It was a Sabbath-day meeting held on April 3, 1836, in the Kirtland Temple in Ohio, seven days after it was dedicated. Joseph Smith described this great moment in the history of the world in a simple way. Much of his account is recorded in Doctrine and Covenants section 110:

"In the afternoon, I assisted the other Presidents in distributing the Lord's Supper to the Church, receiving it from the Twelve, whose privilege it was to officiate at the sacred desk this day. After having performed this service to my brethren, I retired to the pulpit, the veils being dropped, and bowed myself, with Oliver Cowdery, in solemn and silent prayer. After rising from prayer, the following vision was opened to both of us."[1]

"The veil was taken from our minds, and the eyes of our understanding were opened.

"We saw the Lord standing upon the breastwork of the pulpit, before us; and under his feet was a paved work of pure gold, in color like amber.

"His eyes were as a flame of fire; the hair of his head was white like the pure snow; his countenance shone above the brightness of the sun; and his voice was as the sound of the rushing of great waters, even the voice of Jehovah, saying:

"I am the first and the last; I am he who liveth, I am he who was slain; I am your advocate with the Father.

"Behold, your sins are forgiven you; you are clean before me; therefore, lift up your heads and rejoice.

"Let the hearts of your brethren rejoice, and let the hearts of all my people rejoice, who have, with their might, built this house to my name.

"For behold, I have accepted this house, and my name shall be here; and I will manifest myself to my people in mercy in this house.

"Yea, I will appear unto my servants, and speak unto them with mine own voice, if my people will keep my commandments, and do not pollute this holy house.

"Yea the hearts of thousands and tens of thousands shall greatly rejoice in consequence of the blessings which shall be poured out, and the endowment with which my servants have been endowed in this house.

"And the fame of this house shall spread to foreign lands; and this is the beginning of the blessing which shall be poured out upon the heads of my people. Even so. Amen.

"After this vision closed, the heavens were again opened unto us; and Moses appeared before us, and committed unto us the keys of the gathering of Israel from the four parts of the earth, and the leading of the ten tribes from the land of the north.

"After this, Elias appeared, and committed the dispensation of the gospel of Abraham, saying that in us and our seed all generations after us should be blessed.

"After this vision had closed, another great and glorious vision burst upon us; for Elijah the prophet, who was taken to heaven without tasting death, stood before us, and said:

"Behold, the time has fully come, which was spoken of by the mouth of Malachi—testifying that he [Elijah] should be sent, before the great and dreadful day of the Lord come—

"To turn the hearts of the fathers to the children, and the children to the fathers, lest the whole earth be smitten with a curse—

"Therefore, the keys of this dispensation are committed into your hands; and by this ye may know that the great and dreadful day of the Lord is near, even at the doors."[2]

Now, I had read that account many times. The Holy Ghost had confirmed to me that the account was true. But as I studied and prepared for this conference, I came to see more clearly the power of the Lord to lead in detail His disciples in His work.

Seven years before Moses committed to Joseph the keys of the gathering of Israel in the Kirtland Temple, "Joseph learned from the title page of the Book of Mormon that its purpose was to 'show unto the remnant of the house of Israel . . . that they may know the covenants of the Lord, that they are not cast off forever.' In 1831, the Lord told Joseph that the gathering of Israel would commence in Kirtland, 'And from thence [Kirtland], whosoever I will shall go forth among all nations . . . for Israel shall be saved, and I will lead them.'"[3]

Although missionary work was needed to gather Israel, the Lord inspired His leaders to teach the Twelve, who became some of our early missionaries, "Remember you are not to go to other nations, till you receive your endowment."[4]

It seems that the Kirtland Temple was important to the Lord's step-by-step plan for at least two reasons: First, Moses waited until the temple was completed to restore the keys of the gathering of Israel. And second, President Joseph Fielding Smith taught that "the Lord commanded the Saints to build a temple [the Kirtland Temple] in which he could reveal the keys of authority and where the apostles could be endowed and prepared to prune his vineyard for the last time."[5] Although the temple endowment as we know it today wasn't administered in the Kirtland Temple, in fulfillment of prophecy, preparatory temple ordinances began to be introduced there, along with an outpouring of spiritual manifestations which armed those called on missions with the promised endowment of "power from on high"[6] that led to a great gathering through missionary service.

After the keys of the gathering of Israel were committed to Joseph, the Lord inspired the Prophet to send out members of the Twelve on missions. As I studied, it became clear to me that the Lord had prepared in detail the way for the Twelve to go on missions abroad where people had been prepared to believe and sustain them. In time, thousands would, through them, be brought into the Lord's restored Church.

According to our records, it is estimated that between 7,500 and 8,000 were baptized during the two missions of the Twelve to the British Isles. This laid the foundation for missionary work in Europe. By the end of the 19th century, some 90,000 had gathered to America, with the most of these coming from the British Isles and Scandinavia.[7] The Lord had inspired Joseph and those faithful missionaries who went to work to achieve a harvest that must have, at the time, seemed beyond them. But the Lord, with His perfect foresight and preparation, made it possible.

You remember the apparently simple and almost poetic language from section 110 of the Doctrine and Covenants:

"Behold, the time has fully come, which was spoken of by the mouth of Malachi—testifying that he [Elijah] should be sent, before the great and dreadful day of the Lord come—

"To turn the hearts of the fathers to the children, and the children to the fathers, lest the whole earth be smitten with a curse—

"Therefore, the keys of this dispensation are committed into your hands; and by this ye may know that the great and dreadful day of the Lord is near, even at the doors."[8]

I testify that the Lord saw far into the future and how He would lead us to help Him accomplish His purposes in the last days.

While I was serving in the Presiding Bishopric many years ago, I was charged with overseeing the design and development group that created what we named FamilySearch. I am careful to say that I "oversaw" its creation rather than saying I "directed" it. Many brilliant people left careers and came to build what the Lord wanted.

The First Presidency had set a goal of reducing the duplication of ordinances. Their major concern was our being unable to know whether a person's ordinances had already been performed. For years—or what seemed like years—the First Presidency asked me, "When will you have it done?"

With prayer, diligence, and the personal sacrifice of people of great ability, the task was accomplished. It came step by step. The first task was to make FamilySearch user-friendly for those who were not comfortable with computers. More changes came, and I know they will continue to come, for whenever we proceed to resolve one inspired problem, we open the door for further revelation for advancements at least equally important but not yet seen. Even today, FamilySearch is becoming what the Lord needs for part of His Restoration—and not just for avoiding duplication of ordinances.

The Lord let us make improvements to help people gain feelings of familiarity and even love for their ancestors and complete their temple ordinances. Now, as the Lord surely knew would happen, young people are becoming computer mentors to their parents and ward members. All have found great joy in this service.

The spirit of Elijah is changing the hearts of young and old, children and parents, grandchildren and grandparents. Temples will soon again be happily scheduling baptismal opportunities and other sacred ordinances. The desire to serve our ancestors and the bonding of parents and children are growing.

The Lord saw it all coming. He planned for it, step by step, as He has done with other changes in His Church. He has raised up and prepared faithful people who choose to do hard things well. He has always been lovingly patient in helping us learn "line upon line, precept upon precept, here a little and there a little."[9] He is firm in the timing and the sequence of His intentions, yet He ensures that sacrifice often brings continuing blessings that we did not foresee.

I close by expressing my gratitude to the Lord—He who inspired President Nelson to invite me to make a sacrifice to prepare for this conference. Every hour and every prayer during my preparation brought a blessing.

I invite all who hear this message or read these words to have faith that the Lord is leading the Restoration of His gospel and His Church. He goes before us. He knows the future perfectly. He invites you to the work. He joins you in it. He has in place a plan for your service. And even as you sacrifice, you will feel joy as you help others rise to be ready for His coming.

I testify to you that God the Father lives. Jesus is the Christ. This is His Church. He knows and loves you. He guides you. He has prepared the way for you. In the sacred name of Jesus Christ, amen.

Notes
1. Doctrine and Covenants 110, section heading; see also Joseph Smith, "History, 1838–1856, volume B-1 [1 September 1834–2 November 1838]," Apr. 3, 1836, 727, josephsmithpapers.org.
2. Doctrine and Covenants 110:1–16.
3. Karl Ricks Anderson, *The Savior in Kirtland: Personal Accounts of Divine Manifestations* (2012), 276; Doctrine and Covenants 38:33.
4. Given in the apostolic charge administered by Oliver Cowdery, in "Minute Book 1," Feb. 21, 1835, 162, josephsmithpapers.org.
5. Joseph Fielding Smith, *Doctrines of Salvation,* comp. Bruce R. McConkie (1955), 2:234.
6. Doctrine and Covenants 38:32.
7. See James B. Allen, Ronald K. Esplin, and David J. Whittaker, *Men with a Mission: The Quorum of the Twelve Apostles in the British Isles, 1837–1841* (1992), 53, 302; Brandon S. Plewe, ed., *Mapping Mormonism: An Atlas of Latter-day Saint History* (2012), 104.
8. Doctrine and Covenants 110:14–16.
9. 2 Nephi 28:30.

THE MELCHIZEDEK PRIESTHOOD AND THE KEYS

PRESIDENT DALLIN H. OAKS
First Counselor in the First Presidency

I have chosen to speak further about the priesthood of God, the subject already addressed by three earlier speakers who taught us about how the priesthood blesses the lives of women, young women, and young men.

The priesthood is a divine power and authority held in trust to be used for God's work for the benefit of all of His children. *Priesthood* is not those who have been ordained to a priesthood office or those who exercise its authority. Men who hold the priesthood are not the priesthood. While we should not refer to ordained men as *the priesthood*, it is appropriate to refer to them as *holders* of the priesthood.

The power of the priesthood exists both in the Church and in the family organization. But priesthood power and priesthood authority function differently in the Church than they do in the family. All of this is according to the principles the Lord has established. The purpose of God's plan is to lead His children to eternal life. Mortal families are essential to that plan. The Church exists to provide the doctrine, the authority, and the ordinances necessary to perpetuate family relationships into the eternities. Thus, the family organization and the Church of Jesus Christ have a mutually reinforcing relationship. The blessings of the priesthood—such as the fulness of the gospel and ordinances like baptism, confirmation and receiving the gift of the Holy Ghost, the temple endowment, and eternal marriage—are available to men and women alike.[1]

The priesthood we speak of here is the Melchizedek Priesthood, restored at the beginning of the Restoration of the gospel. Joseph Smith and Oliver Cowdery were ordained by Peter, James, and John, who declared themselves "as possessing the keys of the kingdom, and of the dispensation of the fulness of times" (Doctrine and Covenants 128:20). These senior Apostles received that authority from the Savior Himself. All other authorities or offices in the priesthood are appendages to the Melchizedek Priesthood (see Doctrine and Covenants 107:5), for it "holds the right of presidency, and has power and authority over all the offices in the church in all ages of the world" (Doctrine and Covenants 107:8).

In the Church the authority of the greater priesthood, the Melchizedek Priesthood, and the lesser or Aaronic Priesthood is exercised under the direction of a priesthood leader, like a bishop or president, who holds the keys of that priesthood. To understand the exercise of priesthood authority in the Church, we must understand the principle of priesthood keys.

The Melchizedek Priesthood keys of the kingdom were conferred by Peter, James, and John, but that did not complete the restoration of priesthood keys. Some keys of the priesthood came later. Following the dedication of the first temple of this dispensation in Kirtland, Ohio, three prophets—Moses, Elias, and Elijah—restored "the keys of this dispensation," including keys pertaining to the gathering of Israel and the work of the temples of the Lord (see Doctrine and Covenants 110), as President Eyring has just described so persuasively.

The most familiar example of the function of keys is in the performance of priesthood ordinances. An ordinance is a solemn act signifying the making of covenants and the promising of blessings. In the Church all ordinances are performed under the authorization of the priesthood leader who holds the keys for that ordinance.

An ordinance is most commonly officiated by persons who have been ordained to an office in the priesthood acting under the direction of one who holds priesthood keys. For example, the holders of the various offices of the Aaronic Priesthood officiate in the ordinance of the sacrament under the keys and direction of the bishop, who holds the keys of the Aaronic Priesthood. The same principle applies to the priesthood ordinances in which women officiate in the temple. Though women do not hold an office in the priesthood, they perform sacred temple ordinances under the authorization of the president of the temple, who holds the keys for the ordinances of the temple.

Another example of priesthood authority under the direction of one who holds the keys are the teachings of men and women called to teach the gospel, whether in classes in their home wards or in the mission field. Other examples are those who hold leadership positions in the ward and exercise priesthood authority in their leadership by reason of their callings and under the setting apart and direction of the priesthood leader who holds the keys in the ward or the stake. This is how the authority and power of the priesthood is exercised and enjoyed in The Church of Jesus Christ of Latter-day Saints.[2]

Priesthood authority is also exercised and its blessings realized in the families of Latter-day Saints. By families I mean a priesthood-holding man and a woman who are married and their children. I also include the variations from the ideal relationships such as caused by death or divorce.

The principle that priesthood authority can be exercised only under the direction of the one who holds the keys for that function is fundamental in the Church, but this does not apply in the family. For example, a father presides and exercises the priesthood in his family by the authority of the priesthood he holds. He has no need to have the direction or approval of one holding priesthood keys in order to perform his various family functions. These include counseling the members of his family, holding family meetings, giving priesthood blessings to his wife and children, or giving healing blessings to family members or others.[3] Church authorities teach family members but do not direct the exercise of priesthood authority in the family.

The same principle applies when a father is absent and a mother is the family leader. She presides in her home and is instrumental in bringing the power and blessings of the priesthood into her family through her endowment and sealing in the temple. While she is not authorized to give the priesthood blessings that can be given only by a person holding a certain office in the priesthood, she can perform all of the other functions of family leadership. In doing so, she exercises the power of the priesthood for the benefit of the children over whom she presides in her position of leadership in the family.[4]

If fathers would magnify their priesthood in their own family, it would further the mission of the Church as much as anything else they might do. Fathers who hold the Melchizedek Priesthood should exercise their authority "by persuasion, by long-suffering, by gentleness and meekness, and by love unfeigned" (Doctrine and Covenants 121:41). That high standard for the exercise of all priesthood authority is most important in the family. Holders of the priesthood should also keep the commandments so they will have the power of the priesthood to give blessings to their family members. They should cultivate loving family relationships so that family members will want to ask them for blessings. And parents should encourage more priesthood blessings in the family.[5]

In these conference meetings, as we seek brief shelter from our mortal concerns with a devastating pandemic, we have been taught great principles of eternity. I encourage each of us to have our eye "single" to receive these truths of eternity so that our bodies "shall be full of light" (3 Nephi 13:22).

In His sermon to multitudes recorded in the Bible and in the Book of Mormon, the Savior taught that mortal bodies can be full of light or full of darkness. We, of course, want to be filled with light, and our Savior taught us how we can make this happen. We should listen to messages about the truths of eternity. He used the example of our eye, through which we take light into our bodies. If our "eye be single"—in other words, if we are concentrating on receiving eternal light and understanding—He explained, "thy whole body shall be full of light" (Matthew 6:22; 3 Nephi 13:22). But if our "eye be evil"—that is, if we look for evil and take that into our bodies—He warned, "thy whole body shall be full of darkness" (verse 23). In other words, the light or darkness in our bodies depends on how we see—or receive—the eternal truths we are taught.

We should follow the Savior's invitation to seek and ask to understand the truths of eternity. He promises that our Father in

Heaven is willing to teach everyone the truths they seek (see 3 Nephi 14:8). If we desire this and have our eye single to receive them, the Savior promises that the truths of eternity "shall be opened" unto us (see 3 Nephi 14:7–8).

In contrast, Satan is anxious to confuse our thinking or to lead us astray on important matters like the operations of the priesthood of God. The Savior warned of such "false prophets, who come to you in sheep's clothing, but inwardly they are ravening wolves" (3 Nephi 14:15). He gave us this test to help us choose the truth from among different teachings that might confuse us: "Ye shall know them by their fruits," He taught (3 Nephi 14:16). "A good tree cannot bring forth evil fruit, neither [can] a corrupt tree bring forth good fruit" (verse 18). Therefore, we should look to the results—"the fruits"— of principles that are taught and the persons who teach them. That is the best answer to many of the objections we hear against the Church and its doctrines and policies and leadership. Follow the test the Savior taught. Look to the fruits—the results.

When we think of the fruits of the gospel and the restored Church of Jesus Christ, we rejoice in how the Church, in the lifetimes of its living members, has expanded from local congregations in the Intermountain West to where a majority of its more than 16 million members reside in nations other than the United States. With that growth, we have felt increases in the Church's capacity to assist its members. We assist in keeping the commandments, in fulfilling responsibilities to preach the restored gospel, in gathering Israel, and in building temples throughout the world.

We are led by a prophet, President Russell M. Nelson, whose leadership the Lord has used to achieve the progress we have felt during all of the more than two years of his leadership. Now we will be blessed to hear from President Nelson, who will teach us how to further our progress in this restored Church of Jesus Christ in these challenging times.

I testify of the truth of these things and join you in praying for our prophet, from whom we will next hear, in the name of Jesus Christ, amen.

Notes

1. See Dallin H. Oaks, "Priesthood Authority in the Family and the Church," *Ensign* or *Liahona,* Nov. 2005, 24–27.
2. See Russell M. Nelson, "Spiritual Treasures," *Ensign* or *Liahona,* Nov. 2019, 76–79; Dallin H. Oaks, "Priesthood Authority in the Family and the Church," 24–27; Dallin H. Oaks, "The Keys and Authority of the Priesthood," *Ensign* or *Liahona,* May 2014, 49–52.
3. See Dallin H. Oaks, "The Powers of the Priesthood," *Ensign* or *Liahona,* May 2018, 65–68.
4. See Russell M. Nelson, "Spiritual Treasures," 76–79.
5. See Russell M. Nelson, "Ministering with the Power and Authority of God," *Ensign* or *Liahona,* May 2018, 68–75; Dallin H. Oaks, "The Powers of the Priesthood," 65–68.

OPENING THE HEAVENS FOR HELP
PRESIDENT RUSSELL M. NELSON
President of The Church of Jesus Christ of Latter-day Saints

What a unique and wonderful session this has been! Thank you, dear Laudy and Enzo. You represented the magnificent young women and young men of the Church so very well.

My dear brothers and sisters, we have heard much today about the Restoration of the Church—the very Church that our Savior, Jesus Christ, established during His earthly ministry. That Restoration began 200 years ago this spring when God the Father and His Son, Jesus Christ, appeared to the young Joseph Smith.

Ten years after this transcendent vision, the Prophet Joseph Smith and five others were called as founding members of the Lord's restored Church.

From that small group assembled on April 6, 1830, has come a global organization of more than 16 million members. The good this Church accomplishes around the world to alleviate human suffering and provide uplift for humankind is widely known. But its prime purpose is to help men, women, and children follow the Lord Jesus Christ, keep His commandments, and qualify for the greatest of all blessings—that of eternal life with God and their loved ones.[1]

As we commemorate the event that was launched in 1820, it is important to remember that while we revere Joseph Smith as a prophet of God, this is not the church of Joseph Smith, nor is it the church of Mormon. This is the Church of Jesus Christ. He decreed exactly what His Church should be called: "For thus shall my church be called in the last days, even The Church of Jesus Christ of Latter-day Saints."[2]

I have spoken previously about a needed course correction in the way we refer to the name of the Church.[3] Since that time, much has been done to accomplish this correction. I am very grateful to President M. Russell Ballard and the entire Quorum of the Twelve Apostles, who have done so much to lead these efforts as well as those related to another initiative that I will announce this evening.

Church leaders and departments, related entities, and millions of members—and others—now use the correct name of the Church. The Church's official style guide has been adjusted. The Church's principal website is now ChurchofJesusChrist.org. Addresses for email, domain names, and social media channels have been updated. Our beloved choir is now the Tabernacle Choir at Temple Square.

We have gone to these extraordinary efforts because when we remove the Lord's name from the name of *His* Church, we inadvertently remove *Him* as the central focus of our worship and our lives. When we take the Savior's name upon us at baptism, we commit to witness, by our words, thoughts, and actions, that Jesus is the Christ.[4]

Previously, I promised that if we would "do our best to restore the correct name of the Lord's Church," He would "pour down His power and blessings upon the heads of the Latter-day Saints, the likes of which we have never seen."[5] I renew that promise today.

To help us remember Him and to identify The Church of Jesus Christ of Latter-day Saints as the *Lord's Church,* we are pleased to introduce a symbol that will signify the central place of Jesus Christ in His Church.

This symbol includes the name of the Church contained within a cornerstone. Jesus Christ is the chief cornerstone.[6]

At the center of the symbol is a representation of Thorvaldsen's marble statue the *Christus.* It portrays the resurrected, *living* Lord reaching out to embrace all who will come unto Him.

Symbolically, Jesus Christ is standing under an arch. The arch reminds us of the resurrected Savior emerging from the tomb on the third day following His Crucifixion.

This symbol should feel familiar to many, as we have long identified the restored gospel with the *living,* resurrected Christ.

The symbol will now be used as a visual identifier for official literature, news, and events of the Church.[7] It will remind all that this is the Savior's Church and that all we do as members of His Church centers on Jesus Christ and His gospel.

Now, my dear brothers and sisters, tomorrow is Palm Sunday,

as Elder Gong has so eloquently taught. Then we enter the special week that culminates with Easter. As followers of Jesus Christ, living in a day when the COVID-19 pandemic has put the whole world in commotion, let us not just talk of Christ or preach of Christ or employ a symbol representing Christ.

Let us put our faith in the Lord Jesus Christ into action!

As you know, members of the Church observe the law of the fast one day each month.

The doctrine of fasting is ancient. It has been practiced by biblical heroes from the earliest days. Moses, David, Ezra, Nehemiah, Esther, Isaiah, Daniel, Joel, and many others fasted and preached of fasting.[8] Through Isaiah's writings, the Lord said: "Is *not* this the fast that I have chosen? to loose the bands of wickedness, to undo the heavy burdens, and to let the oppressed go free?"[9]

The Apostle Paul admonished Saints in Corinth to "give yourselves to fasting and prayer."[10] The Savior Himself declared that certain things go "not out *but* by prayer and fasting."[11]

I said recently in a social media video that "as a physician and surgeon, I have great admiration for medical professionals, scientists, and all who are working around the clock to curb the spread of COVID-19."[12]

Now, as President of The Church of Jesus Christ of Latter-day Saints and an Apostle of Jesus Christ, I *know* that God "has all power, all wisdom, and all understanding; he comprehendeth all things, and he is a merciful Being, even unto salvation, to those who will repent and believe on his name."[13]

So, during times of deep distress, as when illness reaches pandemic proportions, the most natural thing for us to do is to call upon our Heavenly Father and His Son—the Master Healer—to show forth Their marvelous power to bless the people of the earth.

In my video message, I invited all to join in fasting on Sunday, March 29, 2020. Many of you may have seen the video and joined in the fast. Some may have not. Now we still need help from heaven.

So tonight, my dear brothers and sisters, in the spirit of the sons of Mosiah, who gave themselves to much fasting and prayer,[14] and as part of our April 2020 general conference, I am calling for another worldwide fast. For all whose health may permit, let us fast, pray, and unite our faith once again. Let us prayerfully plead for relief from this global pandemic.

I invite *all,* including those not of our faith, to fast and pray on Good Friday, April 10, that the present pandemic may be controlled, caregivers protected, the economy strengthened, and life normalized.

How do we fast? Two meals or a period of 24 hours is customary. But you decide what would constitute a sacrifice for you, as you remember the supreme sacrifice the Savior made for you. Let us unite in pleading for healing throughout the world.

Good Friday would be *the* perfect day to have our Heavenly Father and His Son hear *us!*

Dear brothers and sisters, I express my deep love for you, along with my testimony of the divinity of the work in which we are engaged. This *is* The Church of Jesus Christ of Latter-day Saints. He stands at its head and directs all that we do. I know that He will respond to the pleadings of His people. I so testify in the sacred name of Jesus Christ, amen.

Notes

1. See Doctrine and Covenants 14:7.
2. Doctrine and Covenants 115:4.
3. See Russell M. Nelson, "The Correct Name of the Church," *Ensign* or *Liahona,* Nov. 2018, 87–89.
4. See Russell M. Nelson, "The Correct Name of the Church," 88.
5. Russell M. Nelson, "The Correct Name of the Church," 89.
6. See Ephesians 2:20.
7. To respect the sacred nature of the Church symbol and preserve legal protection, the Church's official symbol is to be used only as approved by the First Presidency and Quorum of the Twelve Apostles. Further information may be obtained by contacting the Church's Intellectual Property Office at cor-intellectualproperty@ChurchofJesusChrist.org.
8. See Exodus 34:28; 2 Samuel 12:16; Ezra 10:6; Nehemiah 1:4; Esther 4:16; Isaiah 58:3; Daniel 9:3; Joel 2:12.
9. Isaiah 58:6; emphasis added.
10. 1 Corinthians 7:5.
11. Matthew 17:21; emphasis added.
12. Russell M. Nelson, in "Prophet Invites All to Fast and Pray for Relief from COVID-19," Mar. 26, 2020, newsroom.ChurchofJesusChrist.org.
13. Alma 26:35.
14. See Alma 17:3.

Sunday Morning Session

April 5, 2020

FULFILLMENT OF PROPHECY
ELDER RONALD A. RASBAND
Of the Quorum of the Twelve Apostles

My dear brothers and sisters, I am honored to speak at this historic general conference commemorating Joseph Smith's First Vision of God the Father and His Son, Jesus Christ, in what is, without question, a Sacred Grove. That vision was a magnificent beginning to the Restoration of the gospel and all that unfolded, from the Book of Mormon to the return of priesthood authority and keys, the organization of the Lord's true Church, temples of God, and prophets and apostles who lead the work in these latter days.

By divine design, ancient prophets of God, when moved upon by the Holy Ghost, prophesied of the Restoration and what was to come in our day, the last dispensation and the fulness of times. The very work "fired the souls" of the early seers.[1] Through generations of time, they foretold, dreamed, envisioned, and prophesied of the future of God's kingdom on earth, what Isaiah called "a marvellous work and a wonder."[2]

The prophecies that have been fulfilled by the Restoration of the fulness of the gospel of Jesus Christ, including The Church of Jesus Christ of Latter-day Saints, are many. Today, however, I will highlight only a few of my favorites. These were taught to me by my dear Primary teachers and at the knee of my angel mother.

Daniel, who staved off lions by his faith in the Lord Jesus Christ and the intercession of God's ministering angels, was one who saw our day in vision. Interpreting a dream for Babylonian King Nebuchadnezzar, Daniel prophesied the Lord's Church would rise in the last days as a small stone "cut out of the mountain without hands."[3] "Without hands," meaning by divine intervention, the Lord's Church would increase in magnitude until it fills the whole earth, "never [to] be destroyed . . . [but to] stand for ever."[4]

It is a profound witness that Daniel's words are being fulfilled as members of the Church, from all over the world, are watching and listening to the conference today.

The devoted Apostle Peter described "times of restitution of all things . . . since the world began."[5] The Apostle Paul wrote that in the fulness of times, God would "gather . . . in one all things in Christ,"[6] "Jesus Christ himself being the chief corner stone."[7] I felt those prophecies so strongly when I participated in the dedication of the Rome Italy Temple. All of the prophets and apostles were there bearing testimony of Jesus Christ, the Redeemer of the world, as had Peter and Paul. The Church is a living example of that restitution, brothers and sisters, and our members are witnesses of those divine prophecies long ago.

Joseph of Egypt prophesied that in the latter days "a seer shall the Lord my God raise up, who shall be a choice seer unto the fruit of my loins."[8] "For he shall do [the Lord's] work."[9] Joseph Smith, the prophet of the Restoration, was that seer.

John the Revelator prophesied of an angel of the Almighty bringing together important elements of the Restoration with these words: "And I saw another angel fly in the midst of heaven, having the everlasting gospel to preach unto them that dwell on the earth, and to every nation, and kindred, and tongue, and people."[10] Moroni was that angel. He saw our day as recorded in the Book of Mormon. In repeated appearances, he prepared Joseph Smith for his ministry, including the translation of the Book of Mormon: Another Testament of Jesus Christ.

Other prophets foretold of our day. Malachi spoke of Elijah turning "the heart of the fathers to the children, and the heart of the children to their fathers."[11] Elijah has come, and as a result, today we have 168 temples dotting the earth. Each temple serves worthy members making sacred covenants and receiving blessed ordinances on behalf of themselves and their deceased ancestors. This sacred work described by Malachi is "central to the Creator's plan for the eternal destiny of His children."[12]

We live in that time prophesied; we are the people charged with ushering in the Second Coming of Jesus Christ; we are to gather God's children, those who will hear and embrace the truths, covenants, and promises of the everlasting gospel. President Nelson calls it "*the greatest* challenge, *the greatest* cause, and *the greatest* work on [the] earth today."[13] Of that miracle I bear my witness.

By assignment from President Russell M. Nelson, in February of this year I dedicated the Durban South Africa Temple. It was a day I will remember all my life. I was with members who have come to the gospel as Jeremiah prophesied long ago—"one of a city, and two of a family."[14] The doctrine of Jesus Christ unites all of us—around the world—as sons and daughters of God, as brothers and sisters in the gospel. Regardless of how we look or dress, we are one people with a Father in Heaven whose plan from the beginning was and is for His family to be reunited by making and keeping sacred temple covenants.

To a small gathering of priesthood holders in a schoolhouse in Kirtland, Ohio, in 1834, the Prophet Joseph prophesied, "It is only a little handfull of Priesthood you see here tonight, but this Church will fill North and South America—it will fill the world."[15]

In recent years I have traveled throughout the world to meet the members of the Church. My Brethren of the Quorum of the Twelve have had similar assignments. Still, who can keep up with the schedule of our dear prophet, President Nelson, whose travel in his first two years as President of the Church has taken him to meet with the Saints in 32 countries and U.S. territories[16] to witness of the living Christ.

I remember when I received my mission call as a young man. I wanted to serve in Germany, like my father, brother, and brother-in-law. Not waiting for anyone to get home, I rushed to the mailbox and opened the call. I read that I had been called to the Eastern States Mission, headquartered in New York City. I was disappointed, so I went inside and opened my scriptures for comfort. I began to read in the Doctrine and Covenants: "Behold, and lo, I have much people in this place, in the regions round about; and an effectual door shall be opened in the regions round about in this eastern land."[17] That prophecy, given to the Prophet Joseph Smith in 1833, was a revelation to me. I knew then I had been called to the exact mission the Lord wanted me to serve in. I taught the Restoration and its dramatic beginning when our Father in Heaven spoke to Joseph Smith and said, "This is My Beloved Son. Hear Him!"[18]

Of great significance for the whole Church is the prophecy of Isaiah, given more than 700 years before the birth of Jesus Christ: "And it shall come to pass in the last days, that the mountain of the Lord's house shall be established in the top of the mountains, . . . and all nations shall flow unto it."[19]

In my mind today, I picture millions of our members and friends connected to these proceedings electronically by television, internet, or other means. We are sitting down as if together "in the top of the mountains."[20] It was Brigham Young who spoke the prophetic words "This is the right place."[21] The Saints, some of them my own pioneer ancestors, worked to establish Zion in the Rocky Mountains "through the will and pleasure of him who dictates the nations of the earth."[22]

I stand today on the sacred ground that has drawn millions of visitors. In 2002, Salt Lake City hosted the Winter Olympic Games. The Tabernacle Choir sang at the opening ceremonies, and the Church offered concerts and programs for guests and participants from many, many nations. I will always remember seeing the temple in the background of the nightly news broadcasts worldwide.

Over the years, presidents of the United States, kings, judges, prime ministers, ambassadors, and officials from many lands have come to Salt Lake City and met with our leaders. President Nelson hosted leaders of the National Association for the Advancement of Colored People, a United States organization committed to equal rights without discrimination based on race. I remember standing shoulder to shoulder with these friends and leaders as President Nelson joined them in calling for greater civility and racial harmony in the world.[23]

Many more have come to Temple Square and met in council with Church leaders. For example, this past year, to name just a few, we welcomed the United Nations 68th Civil Society Conference, a global gathering and the first of its kind outside of New York City. We have met with Vietnam's Committee for Religious Affairs and ambassadors from Cuba, the Philippines, Argentina, Romania, Sudan, Qatar, and Saudi Arabia. We also welcomed the secretary general of the Muslim World League.

What I am describing is a fulfillment of Isaiah's prophecy that in the last days, nations shall flow unto "the mountain of the Lord's house."[24] The great Salt Lake Temple stands in the center of that majesty and glory.

It is not the landscape that has drawn people, though our setting is magnificent; it is the essence of pure religion exhibited in the spirit, growth, goodness, and generosity of The Church of Jesus Christ of Latter-day Saints and its people; our love as God loves; our commitment to a higher cause, what Joseph Smith called "the cause of Christ."[25]

We do not know when the Savior will return, but this we do know. We must be prepared in heart and mind, worthy to receive Him, and honored to be part of all that was prophesied so long ago.

I testify that President Russell M. Nelson is the Lord's prophet on the earth, and at his side are Apostles called of God, sustained as prophets, seers, and revelators. And, my dear brothers and sisters, the Restoration continues.

I close with the prophecy of Joseph Smith, words that I testify are true: "No unhallowed hand can stop the work from progressing; persecutions may rage, mobs may combine, armies may assemble, calumny may defame, but the truth of God will go forth boldly, nobly, and independent, till it has penetrated every continent, visited every clime, swept every country, and sounded in every ear, till the purposes of God shall be accomplished, and the Great Jehovah shall say the work is done."[26] I so testify that these prophecies of Joseph Smith are being fulfilled.

I promise as you follow the inspired counsel of our dear prophet, President Russell M. Nelson, his counselors, the Apostles, and other Church leaders, and as you pay heed to the ancient prophets who foretold of our day, you will be filled, deep in your heart and soul, with the spirit and the work of the Restoration. I promise you will see the hand of God in your lives, hear His promptings, and feel His love. In the name of Jesus Christ, with gratitude for the Restoration of His gospel and His Church, in evidence of His matchless love, amen.

Notes

1. *Teachings of Presidents of the Church: Joseph Smith* (2007), 515.
2. Isaiah 29:14.
3. Daniel 2:45; see also Doctrine and Covenants 65:2.
4. Daniel 2:44.
5. Acts 3:21.
6. Ephesians 1:10.
7. Ephesians 2:20.
8. 2 Nephi 3:6.
9. 2 Nephi 3:8.
10. Revelation 14:6.
11. Malachi 4:6.
12. "The Family: A Proclamation to the World," *Ensign* or *Liahona,* May 2017, 145.
13. Russell M. Nelson, "Hope of Israel" (worldwide youth devotional, June 3, 2018), HopeofIsrael.ChurchofJesusChrist.org.
14. Jeremiah 3:14.
15. Joseph Smith, in *Teachings of Presidents of the Church: Wilford Woodruff* (2004), 26.
16. See Valerie Johnson, "President Nelson Became the Prophet 2 Years Ago. What Has Happened Since Then?" *Church News,* Jan. 13, 2020, thechurchnews.com.
17. Doctrine and Covenants 100:3.
18. Joseph Smith—History 1:17.
19. Isaiah 2:2; see also Micah 4:1–2.
20. Isaiah 2:2.
21. The phrase "This is the right place" was first attributed to Brigham Young by Wilford Woodruff while speaking at a Pioneer Day celebration in July 1880 (see "Pioneers' Day," *Deseret Evening News,* July 26, 1880, 2).
22. Brigham Young, Mar. 31, 1861, Historian's Office reports of speeches, 1845–1885, Church History Library, Salt Lake City.
23. See "First Presidency and NAACP Leaders Call for Greater Civility, Racial Harmony," May 17, 2018, newsroom.ChurchofJesusChrist.org.
24. Isaiah 2:2; see also Micah 4:1–2.
25. *Teachings: Joseph Smith,* 352.
26. *Teachings: Joseph Smith,* 142.

THAT THEY MAY SEE

BONNIE H. CORDON
Young Women General President

Brothers and sisters, our hearts have been blessed and renewed by the Spirit we have felt at this conference.

Two hundred years ago, a pillar of light rested on a young man in a grove of trees. In that light, Joseph Smith saw God the Father and His Son, Jesus Christ. Their light drove back the spiritual darkness that covered the earth and pointed the way forward for Joseph Smith—and for all of us. Because of the light revealed that day, we can receive the fulness of blessings available through the Atonement of our Savior, Jesus Christ.

By virtue of the Restoration of His gospel, we can be filled with the light of our Savior. However, that light is not meant for you and me alone. Jesus Christ has called upon us to "let your light so shine before this people, that they may see your good works and glorify your Father who is in heaven."[1] I have come to love the phrase "that they may see." It is an earnest invitation from the Lord to be more intentional about helping others see the path and thereby come unto Christ.

When I was 10 years old, our family had the honor of hosting Elder L. Tom Perry of the Quorum of the Twelve Apostles while he was on assignment in my hometown.

At the close of the day, our family and the Perrys sat down in our living room to enjoy my mother's delicious apple pie while Elder Perry recounted stories about Saints around the world. I was enthralled.

It was getting late when my mother called me into the kitchen and asked a simple question: "Bonnie, did you feed the chickens?"

My heart fell; I had not. Not wanting to leave the presence of an Apostle of the Lord, I suggested the chickens could fast until morning.

My mother replied with a definitive "no." Just then, Elder Perry entered the kitchen and with his booming, enthusiastic voice asked,

"Did I hear someone needs to feed the chickens? Can my son and I join you?"

Oh, what an absolute joy it now became to feed the chickens! I ran to get our large yellow flashlight. Excited, I led out, skipping over the well-worn path to the chicken coop. With flashlight swinging from my hand, we crossed the corn patch and passed through the wheat field.

Reaching the small irrigation ditch that crossed the path, I instinctively jumped over it as I had done many nights before. I was oblivious to Elder Perry's efforts to keep up on a dark, unknown path. My dancing light did not help him see the ditch. Without a steady light to see, he stepped directly in the water and let out a loud groan. Panicked, I turned to see my new friend remove his soaking wet foot from the ditch and shaking the water from his heavy leather shoe.

With a soaked and sloshing shoe, Elder Perry helped me feed the chickens. When we were through, he lovingly instructed, "Bonnie, I need to see the path. I need the light to shine where I am walking."

I was shining my light but not in a way that would help Elder Perry. Now, knowing that he needed my light to safely navigate the path, I focused the flashlight just ahead of his steps and we were able to return home with confidence.

My dear brothers and sisters, for years I've pondered the principle I learned from Elder Perry. The Lord's invitation to let our light so shine is not just about randomly waving a beam of light and making the world generally brighter. It is about focusing our light so others may see the way to Christ. It is gathering Israel *on this side of the veil*—helping others see the next step forward in making and keeping sacred covenants with God.[2]

The Savior testified, "Behold I am the light; I have set an example for you."[3] Let's look at one of His examples.

The woman at the well was a Samaritan who did not know Jesus Christ and was viewed by many as an outcast in her own society. Jesus met her and initiated a conversation. He spoke to her of water.

He then led her to increased light as He declared Himself to be the "living water."⁴

Christ was compassionately aware of her and her needs. He met the woman where she was and started by talking about something familiar and common. If He had stopped there, it would have been a positive encounter. But it would not have resulted in her going to the city to proclaim, "Come, see . . . : is not this the Christ?"⁵ Gradually, through the conversation, she discovered Jesus Christ, and despite her past, she became an instrument of light, shining the way for others to see.⁶

Now let's look at two people who followed the Savior's example of shining light. Recently my friend Kevin was seated next to a business executive at dinner. He worried what to talk about for two hours. Following a prompting, Kevin asked, "Tell me about your family. Where do they come from?"

The gentleman knew little about his heritage, so Kevin pulled out his phone, saying, "I have an app that connects people to their families. Let's see what we can find."

After a lengthy discussion, Kevin's new friend asked, "Why is family so important to your church?"

Kevin answered simply, "We believe that we continue to live after we die. If we identify our ancestors and take their names to a sacred place called a temple, we can perform marriage ordinances that will keep our families together even after death."⁷

Kevin started with something he and his new friend had in common. He then found a way to witness of the Savior's light and love.

The second story is about Ella, a collegiate basketball player. Her example began when she received her mission call while away at school. She chose to open her call in front of her team. They knew almost nothing about the Church of Jesus Christ and didn't understand Ella's desire to serve. She prayed repeatedly to know how to explain her mission call in a way that her teammates might feel the Spirit. Her answer?

"I made a PowerPoint," Ella said, "because I'm just that cool." She told them about the potential of serving in one of 400-plus missions and possibly learning a language. She highlighted the thousands of missionaries already serving. Ella ended with a picture of the Savior and this brief testimony: "Basketball is one of the most important things in my life. I moved across the country and left my family to play for this coach and with this team. The only two things that are more important to me than basketball are my faith and my family."[8]

Now, in case you are thinking, "These are great 1,000-watt examples, but I'm a 20-watt bulb," remember that the Savior testified, "I am the light which ye shall hold up."[9] He reminds us that He will bring the light if we will just point others to Him.

You and I have enough light to share *right now*. We can light the next step to help someone draw nearer to Jesus Christ, and then the next step, and the next.

Ask yourself, "Who needs the light you have to find the path they need but cannot see?"

My dear friends, why is shining our light so important? The Lord has told us that "there are many yet on the earth . . . who are only kept from the truth because they know not where to find it."[10] We can help. We can intentionally shine our light so others may see. We can extend an invitation.[11] We can walk the journey with those who are taking a step toward the Savior, no matter how halting. We can gather Israel.

I testify the Lord will magnify every small effort. The Holy Ghost will prompt us to know what to say and do. Such attempts may require us to step out of our comfort zone, but we can be assured that the Lord will help our light shine.

How grateful I am for the Savior's light, which continues to lead this Church through revelation.

I invite all of us to follow the example of Jesus Christ and be compassionately aware of those around us. Look and pray for opportunities to let your light shine that others may see the way to Jesus Christ. His promise is great: "He that followeth me shall not walk in darkness, but shall have the light of life."[12] I testify that our

Savior, Jesus Christ, is the way, the truth, the life, light, and love of the world. In the name of Jesus Christ, amen.

Notes

1. 3 Nephi 12:16.
2. See Russell M. Nelson, "Hope of Israel" (worldwide youth devotional, June 3, 2018), HopeofIsrael.ChurchofJesusChrist.org.
3. 3 Nephi 18:16.
4. See John 4:9–30.
5. John 4:29.
6. See Robert and Marie Lund, "The Savior's Respect for Women," *Ensign,* Mar. 2015, 50–55; *Liahona,* Mar. 2015, 32–36.
7. Personal correspondence.
8. Personal correspondence.
9. 3 Nephi 18:24.
10. Doctrine and Covenants 123:12.
11. See Dieter F. Uchtdorf, "Missionary Work: Sharing What Is in Your Heart," *Ensign* or *Liahona,* May 2019, 15–18.
12. John 8:12.

A PERFECT BRIGHTNESS OF HOPE

ELDER JEFFREY R. HOLLAND
Of the Quorum of the Twelve Apostles

Last October, President Russell M. Nelson invited us to look *ahead* to this April 2020 conference by each of us in our own way looking *back* to see the majesty of God's hand in restoring the gospel of Jesus Christ. Sister Holland and I took that prophetic invitation seriously. We imagined ourselves living in the early 1800s, looking at the religious beliefs of that day. In that imagined setting, we asked ourselves, "What's missing here? What do we wish we had? What do we *hope* God will provide in response to our spiritual longing?"

Well, for one thing, we realized that two centuries ago we would have dearly hoped for the restoration of a truer concept of God than most in that day had, hidden as He often seemed to be behind centuries of error and misunderstanding. To borrow a phrase from William Ellery Channing, a prominent religious figure of the day, we would have looked for the "parental character of God," which Channing considered "the first great doctrine of Christianity."[1] Such a doctrine would have recognized Deity as a caring Father in Heaven, rather than a harsh judge dispensing stern justice or as an absentee landlord who had once been engaged in earthly matters but was now preoccupied somewhere else in the universe.

Yes, our hopes in 1820 would have been to find God speaking and guiding as openly in the present as He did in the past, a true Father, in the most loving sense of that word. He certainly would *not* have been a cold, arbitrary autocrat who predestined a select few for salvation and then consigned the rest of the human family to damnation. No, He would be one whose every action, by divine declaration, would be "for the benefit of the world; for he loveth the world"[2] and every inhabitant in it. That love would be His ultimate reason for sending Jesus Christ, His Only Begotten Son, to the earth.[3]

Speaking of Jesus, had we lived in those first years of the 19th century, we would have realized with great alarm that doubts about the reality of the Savior's life and Resurrection were beginning to take significant hold within Christendom. Therefore, we would have hoped for evidence to come to the whole world that would confirm the biblical witness that Jesus *is* the Christ, the literal Son of God, Alpha and Omega, and the only Savior this world will ever know. It would have been among our dearest hopes that other scriptural evidence be brought forward, something that could constitute another testament of Jesus Christ, enlarging and enhancing our knowledge of His miraculous birth, wondrous ministry, atoning sacrifice, and glorious Resurrection. Truly such a document would be "righteousness [sent] down out of heaven; and truth [sent] forth out of the earth."[4]

Observing the Christian world in that day, we would have hoped to find someone authorized by God with true priesthood authority who could baptize us, bestow the gift of the Holy Ghost, and administer all gospel ordinances necessary for exaltation. In 1820, we would have hoped to see fulfilled the eloquent promises of Isaiah, Micah, and other ancient prophets regarding the return of the majestic house of the Lord.[5] We would have thrilled to see the glory of holy temples established again, with the Spirit, the ordinances, the power, and the authority to teach eternal truths, heal personal wounds, and bind families together forever. I would have looked anywhere and everywhere to find someone authorized to say to me and my beloved Patricia that our marriage in such a setting was sealed for time and all eternity, never to hear or have imposed on us the haunting curse "until death do you part." I know that "in [our] Father's house are many mansions,"[6] but, speaking personally, if I were to be so fortunate as to inherit one of them, it could be no more to me than a decaying shack if Pat and our children were not with me to share that inheritance. And for our ancestors, some of whom lived and died anciently without even hearing the name of Jesus Christ, we would have hoped for that most just and merciful of biblical concepts to be restored—the practice of the living offering up saving ordinances on behalf of their kindred dead.[7] No practice I can imagine would demonstrate with more splendor a loving

God's concern for every one of His earthly children no matter when they lived nor where they died.

Well, our 1820 list of hopes could go on, but perhaps the most important message of the Restoration is that such hopes would *not* have been in vain. Beginning in the Sacred Grove and continuing to this day, these desires began to be clothed in reality and became, as the Apostle Paul and others taught, true anchors to the soul, sure and steadfast.[8] What was once only hoped for has now become history.

Thus our look back at 200 years of God's goodness to the world. But what of our look ahead? We still have hopes that have *not* yet been fulfilled. Even as we speak, we are waging an "all hands on deck" war with COVID-19, a solemn reminder that a virus 1,000 times smaller than a grain of sand[9] can bring entire populations and global economies to their knees. We pray for those who have lost loved ones in this modern plague, as well as for those who are currently infected or at risk. We certainly pray for those who are giving such magnificent health care. When we have conquered this—and we will—may we be equally committed to freeing the world from the virus of hunger, freeing neighborhoods and nations from the virus of poverty. May we hope for schools where students are taught—not terrified they will be shot—and for the gift of personal dignity for every child of God, unmarred by *any* form of racial, ethnic, or religious prejudice. Undergirding all of this is our relentless hope for greater devotion to the two greatest of all commandments: to love God by keeping His counsel and to love our neighbors by showing kindness and compassion, patience and forgiveness.[10] These two divine directives are still—and forever will be—the only real hope we have for giving our children a better world than the one they now know.[11]

In addition to having these global desires, many in this audience today have deeply personal hopes: hope for a marriage to improve, or sometimes just hope for a marriage; hope for an addiction to be conquered; hope for a wayward child to come back; hope for physical and emotional pain of a hundred kinds to cease. Because the

Restoration reaffirmed the foundational truth that God does work in this world, we *can* hope, we *should* hope, even when facing the most insurmountable odds. That is what the scripture meant when Abraham was able to hope against hope[12]—that is, he was able to believe in spite of every reason *not* to believe—that he and Sarah could conceive a child when that seemed utterly impossible. So, I ask, "If so many of our 1820 hopes could begin to be fulfilled with a flash of divine light to a mere boy kneeling in a patch of trees in upstate New York, why should we not hope that righteous desires and Christlike yearnings can still be marvelously, miraculously answered by the God of all hope?" We all need to believe that what we desire in righteousness can someday, someway, somehow yet be ours.

Brothers and sisters, we know what some of the religious deficiencies in the early 19th century were. Furthermore, we know something of today's religious shortcomings that still leave the hunger and hope of some unfulfilled. We know a variety of those dissatisfactions are leading some away from traditional ecclesiastical institutions. We also know, as one frustrated writer wrote, that "many religious leaders [of the day] seem clueless" in addressing this kind of decline, offering in response "a thin gruel of therapeutic deism, cheap symbolic activism, carefully couched heresy, [or sometimes just] uninspiring nonsense"[13]—and all at a time when the world needs so much more, when the rising generation deserves so much more, and when in Jesus's day He offered so much more. As disciples of Christ, we can in our day rise above those ancient Israelites who moaned, "Our bones are dried, and our hope is lost."[14] Indeed, if we finally lose hope, we lose our last sustaining possession. It was over the very gate of hell that Dante wrote a warning to all those traveling through his *Divina Commedia:* "Abandon all hope," he said, "ye who enter here."[15] Truly when hope is gone, what we have left is the flame of the inferno raging on every side.

So, when our backs are to the wall and, as the hymn says, "other helpers fail and comforts flee,"[16] among our most indispensable virtues will be this precious gift of hope linked inextricably to our faith in God and our charity to others.

In this bicentennial year, when we look back to see all we have been given and rejoice in the realization of so many hopes fulfilled, I echo the sentiment of a beautiful young returned sister missionary who said to us in Johannesburg just a few months ago, "[We] did not come this far only to come this far."[17]

Paraphrasing one of the most inspiring valedictories ever recorded in scripture, I say with the prophet Nephi and that young sister:

"My beloved brethren [and sisters], after ye have [received these first fruits of the Restoration], I would ask if all is done? Behold, I say unto you, Nay. . . .

" . . . Ye must press forward with a steadfastness in Christ, *having a perfect brightness of hope,* and a love of God and of all men. . . . If ye shall[,] . . . saith the Father: Ye shall have eternal life."[18]

I give thanks, my brothers and sisters, for all we have been given in this last and greatest of all dispensations, the dispensation of the restored gospel of Jesus Christ. The gifts and blessings that flow from that gospel mean everything to me—everything—so in an effort to thank my Father in Heaven for them, I have "promises to keep, and miles to go before I sleep, and miles to go before I sleep."[19] May we press forward with love in our hearts, walking in the "brightness of hope"[20] that lights the path of holy anticipation we have been on now for 200 years. I testify that the future is going to be as miracle-filled and bountifully blessed as the past has been. We have every reason to hope for blessings even greater than those we have already received because this is the work of Almighty God, this is the Church of continuing revelation, this is the gospel of Christ's unlimited grace and benevolence. I bear witness to all of these truths and so much more in the name of Jesus Christ, amen.

Notes
1. "The Essence of the Christian Religion," in *The Works of William E. Channing* (1888), 1004.
2. 2 Nephi 26:24.
3. See John 3:16–17.
4. Moses 7:62.
5. See Isaiah 2:1–3; Ezekiel 37:26; Micah 4:1–3; Malachi 3:1.
6. John 14:2.
7. See 1 Corinthians 15:29; Doctrine and Covenants 128:15–17.

8. See Hebrews 6:19; Ether 12:4.
9. See "Examination and Description of Soil Profiles," in *Soil Survey Manual,* ed. C. Ditzler, K. Scheffe, and H. C. Monger (2017), nrcs.usda.gov.
10. See Matthew 22:36–40; Mark 12:29–33; see also Leviticus 19:18; Deuteronomy 6:1–6.
11. See Ether 12:4.
12. See Romans 4:18.
13. R. J. Snell, "Quiet Hope: A New Year's Resolution," *Public Discourse: The Journal of the Witherspoon Institute,* Dec. 31, 2019, thepublicdiscourse.com.
14. Ezekiel 37:11.
15. This is the phrase as popularly translated. However, the more literal translation is "All hope abandon, ye who enter here" (Dante Alighieri, "The Vision of Hell," in *Divine Comedy,* trans. Henry Francis Cary [1892], canto III, line 9).
16. "Abide with Me!" *Hymns,* no. 166.
17. Judith Mahlangu (multistake conference near Johannesburg, South Africa, Nov. 10, 2019), in Sydney Walker, "Elder Holland Visits Southeast Africa during 'Remarkable Time of Growth,'" *Church News,* Nov. 27, 2019, thechurchnews.com.
18. 2 Nephi 31:19–20; emphasis added.
19. "Stopping by Woods on a Snowy Evening," lines 14–16, in *The Poetry of Robert Frost: The Collected Poems,* ed. Edward Connery Lathem (1969), 225.
20. 2 Nephi 31:20.

"LET THIS HOUSE BE BUILT UNTO MY NAME"
(Doctrine and Covenants 124:40)

ELDER DAVID A. BEDNAR
Of the Quorum of the Twelve Apostles

In the Sacred Grove 200 years ago, young Joseph Smith saw and talked with God, the Eternal Father, and His Son, Jesus Christ. From Them, Joseph learned about the true nature of the Godhead and of ongoing revelation as this supernal vision ushered in the latter-day "dispensation of the fulness of times."[1]

Approximately three years later, in response to earnest prayer on the evening of September 21, 1823, Joseph's bedroom filled with light until it was "lighter than at noonday."[2] A personage appeared at his bedside, called the young boy by name, and declared "he was a messenger sent from the presence of God . . . and that his name was Moroni."[3] He instructed Joseph about the coming forth of the Book of Mormon.

And then Moroni quoted from the book of Malachi in the Old Testament, with a little variation in the language used in the King James Version:

"Behold, I will reveal unto you the Priesthood, by the hand of Elijah the prophet, before the coming of the great and dreadful day of the Lord. . . .

"And he shall plant in the hearts of the children the promises made to the fathers, and the hearts of the children shall turn to their fathers. If it were not so, the whole earth would be utterly wasted at his coming."[4]

Importantly, Moroni's instruction to Joseph Smith about Elijah's mission initiated temple and family history work in the latter days and was a key element in restoring "all things, which God hath spoken by the mouth of all his holy prophets since the world began."[5]

I pray for the assistance of the Holy Ghost as we learn together about the covenants, ordinances, and blessings that are available to us in the temples of The Church of Jesus Christ of Latter-day Saints.

The Return of Elijah

I begin by asking a fundamental question: why was the return of Elijah important?

"We learn from latter-day revelation that Elijah held the sealing power of the Melchizedek Priesthood"[6] and "was the last prophet to do so before the time of Jesus Christ."[7]

The Prophet Joseph Smith explained: "The spirit, power, and calling of Elijah is, that ye have power to hold the key of the . . . *fullness of the Melchizedek Priesthood* . . . ; and to . . . obtain . . . all the ordinances belonging to the kingdom of God, even unto the turning of the hearts of the fathers unto the children, and the hearts of the children unto the fathers, even those who are in heaven."[8]

This sacred sealing authority is necessary so that "whatsoever thou shalt bind on earth shall be bound in heaven: and whatsoever thou shalt loose on earth shall be loosed in heaven."[9]

Joseph further clarified: "How shall God come to the rescue of this generation? He will send Elijah the prophet. . . . Elijah shall reveal the covenants to seal the hearts of the fathers to the children, and the children to the fathers."[10]

Elijah appeared with Moses on the Mount of Transfiguration and conferred this authority upon Peter, James, and John.[11] Elijah also appeared with Moses and Elias on April 3, 1836, in the Kirtland Temple and conferred the same priesthood keys upon Joseph Smith and Oliver Cowdery.[12]

The restoration of the sealing authority by Elijah in 1836 was necessary to prepare the world for the Savior's Second Coming and initiated a greatly increased and worldwide interest in family history research.

Changing, Turning, and Purifying Hearts

The word *heart* is used over 1,000 times in the standard works. This simple but significant word often denotes the inner feelings of an individual. Our hearts—the sum total of our desires, affections, intentions, motives, and attitudes—define who we are and determine what we will become. And the essence of the Lord's work is changing, turning, and purifying hearts through gospel covenants and priesthood ordinances.

We do not build or enter holy temples solely to have a memorable individual or family experience. Rather, the covenants received and the ordinances performed in temples are essential to the sanctifying of our hearts and for the ultimate exaltation of God's sons and daughters.

Planting in the hearts of the children the promises made to the fathers—even Abraham, Isaac, and Jacob—turning the hearts of the children to their own fathers, conducting family history research, and performing vicarious temple ordinances are labors that bless individuals on both sides of the veil. As we become anxiously engaged in this sacred work, we are obeying the commandments to love and serve God and our neighbors.[13] And such selfless service helps us truly to "Hear Him!"[14] and come unto the Savior.[15]

The most sacred covenants and priesthood ordinances are received only in a temple—the house of the Lord. Everything that is learned and all that is done in the temple emphasize the divinity of Jesus Christ and His role in Heavenly Father's great plan of happiness.

From the Inside Out

President Ezra Taft Benson described an important pattern the Redeemer employs in bringing "to pass the immortality and eternal life of man."[16] He said: "The Lord works from the inside out. The world works from the outside in. The world would take people out of the slums. Christ takes the slums out of people, and then they take themselves out of the slums. The world would mold men by changing their environment. Christ changes men, who then change their environment. The world would shape human behavior, but Christ can change human nature."[17]

Covenants and priesthood ordinances are central in the ongoing process of spiritual rebirth and transformation; they are the means whereby the Lord works with each of us *from the inside out.* Covenants that are honored steadfastly, remembered always, and written "with the Spirit of the living God . . . in fleshy tables of the heart"[18] provide purpose and the assurance of blessings in mortality and for eternity. Ordinances that are received worthily and remembered continually open the heavenly channels through which the power of godliness can flow into our lives.

We do not come to the temple to hide from or escape the evils of the world. Rather, we come to the temple to conquer the world of evil. As we invite into our lives the "power of godliness"[19] by receiving priesthood ordinances and making and keeping sacred covenants, we are blessed with strength beyond our own[20] to overcome the temptations and challenges of mortality and to do and become good.

The Fame of This House Shall Spread

The first temple of this dispensation was constructed in Kirtland, Ohio, and dedicated on March 27, 1836.

In a revelation to the Prophet Joseph Smith one week after the dedication, the Lord declared:

"Let the hearts of all my people rejoice, who have, with their might, built this house to my name. . . .

"Yea the hearts of thousands and tens of thousands shall greatly rejoice in consequence of the blessings which shall be poured out, and the endowment with which my servants have been endowed in this house.

"And the fame of this house shall spread to foreign lands; and this is the beginning of the blessing which shall be poured out upon the heads of my people."[21]

Please note the phrases *the hearts of thousands and tens of thousands shall greatly rejoice* and *the fame of this house shall spread to foreign lands.* These were stunning declarations in April of 1836, when the Church had only a relative handful of members and one temple.

Today in 2020, we have 168 operating temples. Forty-nine additional temples are under construction or have been announced. Houses of the Lord are being constructed on the "isles of the sea"[22] and in countries and locations previously considered by many unlikely to warrant a temple.

The endowment ceremony currently is presented in 88 languages and will become available in many additional languages as temples are built to bless more of God's children. In the next 15 years, the number of languages in which temple ordinances will be available likely will double.

This year we will break ground and start construction on 18 temples. In contrast, it took 150 years to build the first 18 temples, from the organization of the Church in 1830 to the dedication of the Tokyo Japan Temple by President Spencer W. Kimball in 1980.

Consider the hastening of temple work that has occurred just during the lifetime of President Russell M. Nelson. When President Nelson was born on September 9, 1924, the Church had six operating temples.

When he was ordained an Apostle on April 7, 1984, 60 years later, 26 temples were operating, an increase of 20 temples in 60 years.

When President Nelson was sustained as President of the Church, 159 temples were operating, an increase of 133 temples in the 34 years during which he served as a member of the Quorum of the Twelve.

Since becoming the President of the Church on January 14, 2018, President Nelson has announced 35 new temples.

Ninety-six percent of the existing temples have been dedicated during President Nelson's lifetime; 84 percent have been dedicated since he was ordained an Apostle.

Always Focus on the Things That Matter Most

As members of the Lord's restored Church, we stand all amazed at the ever-accelerating pace of His work in the latter days. And more temples are coming.

Brigham Young prophesied, "To accomplish this work there will have to be not only one temple but thousands of them, and thousands and tens of thousands of men and women will go into those temples and officiate for people who have lived as far back as the Lord shall reveal."[23]

Understandably, the announcement of each new temple is a source of great joy and a reason to give thanks to the Lord. However, our primary focus should be on the covenants and ordinances that can change our hearts and deepen our devotion to the Savior and not simply on the location or beauty of the building.

The fundamental obligations that rest upon us as members of the Lord's restored Church are (1) to "Hear Him!"[24] and have our own hearts changed through covenants and ordinances and (2) to fulfill joyfully the divinely appointed responsibility to offer temple blessings to the entire human family on both sides of the veil. With the Lord's direction and help, indeed we will fulfill these sacred duties.

The Building Up of Zion

The Prophet Joseph Smith declared:

"The building up of Zion is a cause that has interested the people of God in every age; it is a theme upon which prophets, priests and kings have dwelt with peculiar delight; they have looked forward with joyful anticipation to the day in which we live; and fired with heavenly and joyful anticipations they have sung and written and prophesied of this our day; but they died without the sight; . . . it is left for us to see, participate in and help to roll forward the Latter-day glory."[25]

"The heavenly Priesthood will unite with the earthly, to bring about those great purposes; . . . a work that God and angels have contemplated with delight for generations past; that fired the souls of the ancient patriarchs and prophets; a work that is destined to bring about the destruction of the powers of darkness, the renovation of the earth, the glory of God, and the salvation of the human family."[26]

I solemnly testify that the Father and the Son appeared to Joseph Smith, and Elijah restored the sealing authority. Sacred temple covenants and ordinances can strengthen us and purify our hearts as we

"Hear Him!"[27] and receive the power of godliness in our lives. And I witness that this latter-day work will destroy the powers of darkness and bring about the salvation of the human family. Of these truths I joyfully testify in the sacred name of the Lord Jesus Christ, amen.

Notes

1. Ephesians 1:10.
2. Joseph Smith—History 1:30.
3. Joseph Smith—History 1:33.
4. Joseph Smith—History 1:38–39.
5. Acts 3:21.
6. Bible Dictionary, "Elijah."
7. Guide to the Scriptures, "Elijah."
8. *Teachings of Presidents of the Church: Joseph Smith* (2007), 311; emphasis added.
9. Matthew 16:19; see also Matthew 18:18; Helaman 10:7; Doctrine and Covenants 124:93; 132:46.
10. *Teachings: Joseph Smith,* 313.
11. See Matthew 17:3.
12. See Doctrine and Covenants 110:13–16.
13. See Matthew 22:34–40.
14. Joseph Smith—History 1:17.
15. See Omni 1:26; Moroni 10:30, 32.
16. Moses 1:39.
17. Ezra Taft Benson, "Born of God," *Ensign,* Nov. 1985, 6.
18. 2 Corinthians 3:3.
19. See Doctrine and Covenants 84:20–21.
20. See "Lord, I Would Follow Thee," *Hymns,* no. 220.
21. Doctrine and Covenants 110:6, 9–10.
22. 2 Nephi 29:7.
23. *Teachings of Presidents of the Church: Brigham Young* (1997), 310.
24. Joseph Smith—History 1:17.
25. *Teachings: Joseph Smith,* 186.
26. *Teachings: Joseph Smith,* 514–15.
27. Joseph Smith—History 1:17.

HEAR HIM
PRESIDENT RUSSELL M. NELSON
President of The Church of Jesus Christ of Latter-day Saints

My dear brothers and sisters, how thankful I am that through the use of technology we have been able to meet together and worship on this Sunday morning. How blessed we are to know that the gospel of Jesus Christ has been restored to the earth!

In the past several weeks, most of us have experienced disruptions in our personal lives. Earthquakes, fires, floods, plagues, and their aftermaths have disrupted routines and caused shortages of food, staples, and savings.

Amidst all of this, we commend you and thank you for choosing to hear the word of the Lord during this time of turmoil by joining with us for general conference. The increasing darkness that accompanies tribulation makes the light of Jesus Christ shine ever brighter. Just think of the good each of us can do during this time of global upheaval. Your love of and faith in the Savior may very well be the catalyst for someone to discover the Restoration of the fulness of the gospel of Jesus Christ.

In the past two years, Sister Nelson and I have met with thousands of you around the world. We have convened with you in outdoor arenas and in hotel ballrooms. In each location, I have felt that I was in the presence of the Lord's elect and that I was seeing the gathering of Israel occur before my eyes.

We live in the day that "our forefathers have awaited with anxious expectation."[1] We have front-row seats to *witness live* what the prophet Nephi saw *only in vision,* that "the power of the Lamb of God" would descend "upon the covenant people of the Lord, who were scattered upon all the face of the earth; and they were armed with righteousness and with the power of God in great glory."[2]

You, my brothers and sisters, are among those men, women, and children whom Nephi saw. Think of that!

Regardless of where you live or what your circumstances are, the Lord Jesus Christ is *your* Savior, and God's prophet Joseph Smith is *your* prophet. He was foreordained before the foundation of the earth to be the prophet of this last dispensation, when "nothing shall be withheld"[3] from the Saints. Revelation continues to flow from the Lord during this ongoing process of restoration.

What does it mean for you that the gospel of Jesus Christ has been restored to the earth?

It means that you and your family can be sealed together forever! It means that because you have been baptized by one who has authority from Jesus Christ and have been confirmed a member of His Church, you can enjoy the constant companionship of the Holy Ghost. He will guide and protect you. It means you will never be left comfortless or without access to the power of God to help you. It means that priesthood power can bless you as you receive essential ordinances and make covenants with God and keep them. What an anchor to our souls are these truths, especially during these times when the tempest is raging.

The Book of Mormon chronicles the classic rise and fall of two major civilizations. Their history demonstrates how easy it is for a majority of the people to forget God, reject warnings of the Lord's prophets, and seek power, popularity, and pleasures of the flesh.[4] Repeatedly, past prophets have declared "great and marvelous things unto the people, which they did not believe."[5]

It is no different in our day. Through the years, great and marvelous things have been heard from dedicated pulpits across the earth. Yet most people do *not* embrace these truths—either because they do not know where to look for them[6] or because they are listening to those who do not have the whole truth or because they have rejected truth in favor of worldly pursuits.

The adversary is clever. For millennia he has been making good look evil and evil look good.[7] His messages tend to be loud, bold, and boastful.

However, messages from our Heavenly Father are strikingly different. He communicates simply, quietly, and with such stunning plainness that we cannot misunderstand Him.[8]

For example, whenever He has introduced His Only Begotten

Son to mortals upon the earth, He has done so with remarkably few words. On the Mount of Transfiguration to Peter, James, and John, God said, "This is my beloved Son: hear him."[9] His words to the Nephites in ancient Bountiful were "Behold my Beloved Son, in whom I am well pleased, in whom I have glorified my name—hear ye him."[10] And to Joseph Smith, in that profound declaration that opened this dispensation, God simply said, *"This is My Beloved Son. Hear Him!"*[11]

Now, my dear brothers and sisters, consider the fact that in these three instances just mentioned, just before the Father introduced the Son, the people involved were in a state of fear and, to some degree, desperation.

The Apostles were afraid when they saw Jesus Christ encircled by a cloud on the Mount of Transfiguration.

The Nephites were afraid because they had been through destruction and darkness for several days.

Joseph Smith was in the grips of a force of darkness just before the heavens opened.

Our Father knows that when we are surrounded by uncertainty and fear, what will help us the very most is to hear His Son.

Because when we seek to hear—truly hear—His Son, we will be guided to know what to do in any circumstance.

The very first word in the Doctrine and Covenants is *hearken*.[12] It means "to listen with the intent to obey."[13] To hearken means to "hear Him"—to *hear* what the Savior says and then to *heed* His counsel. In those two words—"Hear Him"—God gives us the pattern for success, happiness, and joy in this life. We are to *hear* the words of the Lord, *hearken* to them, and *heed* what He has told us!

As we seek to be disciples of Jesus Christ, our efforts to *hear Him* need to be ever more intentional. It takes conscious and consistent effort to fill our daily lives with His words, His teachings, His truths.

We simply cannot rely upon information we bump into on social media. With billions of words online and in a marketing-saturated world constantly infiltrated by noisy, nefarious efforts of the adversary, where *can* we go to hear Him?

We can go to the scriptures. They teach us about Jesus Christ and His gospel, the magnitude of His Atonement, and our Father's great plan of happiness and redemption. Daily immersion in the word of God is crucial for spiritual survival, especially in these days of increasing upheaval. As we feast on the words of Christ daily, the words of Christ will tell us how to respond to difficulties we never thought we would face.

We can also *hear Him* in the temple. The house of the Lord *is* a house of learning. There the Lord teaches in His own way. There each ordinance teaches about the Savior. There we learn how to part the veil and communicate more clearly with heaven. There we learn how to rebuke the adversary and draw upon the Lord's priesthood power to strengthen us and those we love. How eager each of us should be to seek refuge there.

When these temporary COVID-19 restrictions are lifted, please schedule regular time to worship and serve in the temple. Every minute of that time will bless you and your family in ways *nothing* else can. Take time to ponder what you hear and feel when you are there. Ask the Lord to teach you how to open the heavens to bless your life and the lives of those you love and serve.

While worshipping in the temple is presently not possible, I invite you to increase your participation in family history, including family history research and indexing. I promise that as you increase your time in temple and family history work, you will increase and improve your ability to hear Him.

We also *hear Him* more clearly as we refine our ability to recognize the whisperings of the Holy Ghost. It has never been more imperative to know how the Spirit speaks to you than right now. In the Godhead, the Holy Ghost is the messenger. He will bring thoughts to your mind which the Father and Son want you to receive. He is the Comforter. He will bring a feeling of peace to your heart. He testifies of truth and will confirm what is true as you hear and read the word of the Lord.

I renew my plea for you to do *whatever* it takes to increase your spiritual capacity to receive personal revelation.

Doing so will help you know how to move ahead with your life, what to do during times of crisis, and how to discern and avoid the temptations and the deceptions of the adversary.

And, finally, we *hear Him* as we heed the words of prophets, seers, and revelators. Ordained Apostles of Jesus Christ always testify of Him. They point the way as we make our way through the heart-wrenching maze of our mortal experiences.

What will happen as you more intentionally hear, hearken, and heed what the Savior has said and what He is saying now through His prophets? I promise that you will be blessed with additional power to deal with temptation, struggles, and weakness. I promise miracles in your marriage, family relationships, and daily work. And I promise that your capacity to feel joy will increase even if turbulence increases in your life.

This April 2020 general conference is our time to commemorate an event that changed the world. As we anticipated this 200th anniversary of Joseph Smith's First Vision, the First Presidency and Council of the Twelve Apostles wondered what *we* might do to commemorate appropriately this singular event.

That theophany initiated the Restoration of the fulness of the gospel of Jesus Christ and ushered in the dispensation of the fulness of times.

We wondered if a monument should be erected. But as we considered the unique historic and international impact of that First Vision, we felt impressed to create a monument not of granite or stone but of words—words of solemn and sacred proclamation—written, not to be carved in "tables of stone" but rather to be etched in the "fleshy tables" of our hearts.[14]

Since the Church was organized, only five proclamations have been issued, with the last being "The Family: A Proclamation to the World," presented by President Gordon B. Hinckley in 1995.

Now as we contemplate this significant time in the history of the world and the Lord's charge to gather scattered Israel in preparation for the Second Coming of Jesus Christ, we, the First Presidency and Council of the Twelve Apostles, issue the following proclamation.

Its title is "The Restoration of the Fulness of the Gospel of Jesus Christ: A Bicentennial Proclamation to the World." It is authored by the First Presidency and the Council of the Twelve Apostles of The Church of Jesus Christ of Latter-day Saints. It is dated April 2020. To prepare for today, I previously recorded this proclamation in the Sacred Grove, where Joseph Smith first saw the Father and the Son.

"We solemnly proclaim that God loves His children in every nation of the world. God the Father has given us the divine birth, the incomparable life, and the infinite atoning sacrifice of His Beloved Son, Jesus Christ. By the power of the Father, Jesus rose again and gained the victory over death. He is our Savior, our Exemplar, and our Redeemer.

"Two hundred years ago, on a beautiful spring morning in 1820, young Joseph Smith, seeking to know which church to join, went into the woods to pray near his home in upstate New York, USA. He had questions regarding the salvation of his soul and trusted that God would direct him.

"In humility, we declare that in answer to his prayer, God the Father and His Son, Jesus Christ, appeared to Joseph and inaugurated the 'restitution of all things' (Acts 3:21) as foretold in the Bible. In this vision, he learned that following the death of the original Apostles, Christ's New Testament Church was lost from the earth. Joseph would be instrumental in its return.

"We affirm that under the direction of the Father and the Son, heavenly messengers came to instruct Joseph and reestablish the Church of Jesus Christ. The resurrected John the Baptist restored the authority to baptize by immersion for the remission of sins. Three of the original twelve Apostles—Peter, James, and John—restored the apostleship and keys of priesthood authority. Others came as well, including Elijah, who restored the authority to join families together forever in eternal relationships that transcend death.

"We further witness that Joseph Smith was given the gift and power of God to translate an ancient record: the Book of Mormon—Another Testament of Jesus Christ. Pages of this sacred text include an account of the personal ministry of Jesus Christ among people in the Western Hemisphere soon after His Resurrection. It teaches of life's purpose and explains the doctrine of Christ, which is central to that purpose. As a companion scripture to the Bible, the Book of Mormon testifies that all human beings are sons and daughters of a loving Father in Heaven, that He has a divine plan for our lives, and that His Son, Jesus Christ, speaks today as well as in days of old.

"We declare that The Church of Jesus Christ of Latter-day Saints, organized on April 6, 1830, is Christ's New Testament Church restored. This Church is anchored in the perfect life of its chief cornerstone, Jesus Christ, and in His infinite Atonement and literal Resurrection. Jesus Christ has once again called Apostles and has given them priesthood authority. He invites all of us to come unto Him and His Church, to receive the Holy Ghost, the ordinances of salvation, and to gain enduring joy.

"Two hundred years have now elapsed since this Restoration was initiated by God the Father and His Beloved Son, Jesus Christ. Millions throughout the world have embraced a knowledge of these prophesied events.

"We gladly declare that the promised Restoration goes forward through continuing revelation. The earth will never again be the same, as God will 'gather together in one all things in Christ' (Ephesians 1:10).

"With reverence and gratitude, we as His Apostles invite all to know—as we do—that the heavens are open. We affirm that God is making known His will for His beloved sons and daughters. We testify that those who prayerfully study the message of the Restoration and act in faith will be blessed to gain their own witness of its divinity and of its purpose to prepare the world for the promised Second Coming of our Lord and Savior, Jesus Christ."

Beloved brothers and sisters, that is our bicentennial proclamation to the world regarding the Restoration of the gospel of Jesus Christ in its fulness. It has been translated into 12 languages. Other languages will soon follow. It will be available immediately on the Church website, from which you may obtain a copy. Study it privately and with your family members and friends. Ponder the truths and think of the impact those truths will have on your life if you will hear them, hearken to them, and heed the commandments and covenants that accompany them.

I know that Joseph Smith is the foreordained prophet whom the Lord chose to open this last dispensation. Through him the Lord's Church was restored to the earth. Joseph sealed his testimony with his blood. How I love and honor him!

God lives! Jesus is the Christ! His Church has been restored! He and His Father, our Heavenly Father, are watching over us. I so testify in the sacred name of Jesus Christ, amen.

Notes
1. Doctrine and Covenants 121:27.
2. 1 Nephi 14:14.
3. Doctrine and Covenants 121:28.
4. See 1 Nephi 22:23.
5. Ether 12:5.
6. See Doctrine and Covenants 123:12.
7. See Isaiah 5:20; 2 Nephi 15:20.
8. See 2 Nephi 25:4; Alma 5:43.
9. Mark 9:7; Luke 9:35.
10. 3 Nephi 11:7.
11. Joseph Smith—History 1:17.
12. See Doctrine and Covenants 1:1.
13. In the Old Testament, the word *hearken* is translated from the Hebrew *shama,* which is a strong verb that means to "listen with the intent to obey." *Hearken* is a scriptural word that occurs in 40 sections of the Doctrine and Covenants.
14. See 2 Corinthians 3:3.

HOSANNA SHOUT

PRESENTED BY PRESIDENT RUSSELL M. NELSON
President of The Church of Jesus Christ of Latter-day Saints

Now, my dear brothers and sisters, as we commemorate Joseph Smith's First Vision of the Father and the Son, we felt that it would be appropriate to rejoice together by participating in the Hosanna Shout.

This sacred shout was first given in this dispensation at the dedication of the Kirtland Temple on March 27, 1836. It is now given at the dedication of each temple. It is a sacred tribute to the Father and the Son, symbolizing the reaction of the multitude when the Savior made His triumphal entry into Jerusalem. It also reaffirms what young Joseph experienced that day in the Sacred Grove—namely, that the Father and the Son are two glorified Beings, whom we worship and praise.

I will now demonstrate how the Hosanna Shout is given. As I do, I invite our colleagues in the media to treat this very sacred observance with dignity and respect.

Each one participating takes a clean white handkerchief, holding it by one corner, and waves it while saying in unison, "Hosanna, Hosanna, Hosanna to God and the Lamb," repeated three times, followed by "Amen, Amen, and Amen." If you do not have a white handkerchief, you may simply wave your hand.

Brothers and sisters, I now invite you to stand and participate in the Hosanna Shout, following which the "Hosanna Anthem" and "The Spirit of God" (*Hymns*, no. 2) will be sung.

Upon a signal from the conductor, please join in singing "The Spirit of God."

Hosanna, Hosanna, Hosanna to God and the Lamb.
Hosanna, Hosanna, Hosanna to God and the Lamb.
Hosanna, Hosanna, Hosanna to God and the Lamb.
Amen, Amen, and Amen.

SUNDAY AFTERNOON SESSION

APRIL 5, 2020

THE GREAT PLAN

PRESIDENT DALLIN H. OAKS
First Counselor in the First Presidency

Even in the midst of unique trials and challenges, we are truly blessed! This general conference has given us an outpouring of the riches and joy of the Restoration of the gospel of Jesus Christ. We have rejoiced in the vision of the Father and the Son that commenced the Restoration. We have been reminded of the miraculous coming forth of the Book of Mormon, whose central purpose is to testify of Jesus Christ and His doctrine. We have been renewed with the joyful reality of revelation—to prophets and to us personally. We have heard precious testimonies of the infinite Atonement of Jesus Christ and of His literal Resurrection. And we have been taught other truths of the fulness of His gospel revealed to Joseph Smith after God the Father declared to that newly called prophet: "This is My Beloved Son. Hear Him!" (Joseph Smith—History 1:17).

We have been affirmed in our knowledge of the restoration of the priesthood and its keys. We have been renewed in our determination to have the Lord's restored Church known by its proper name, The Church of Jesus Christ of Latter-day Saints. And we have been invited to join in fasting and prayer to minimize the present and future effects of a devastating worldwide pandemic. This morning we were inspired by the Lord's living prophet presenting an historic proclamation of the Restoration. We affirm its declaration that "those who prayerfully study the message of the Restoration and act in faith will be blessed to gain their own witness of its divinity and of its purpose to prepare the world for the promised Second Coming of our Lord and Savior, Jesus Christ."[1]

The Plan

All of this is part of a divine plan whose purpose is to enable the children of God to be exalted and become like Him. Referred to in the scriptures as the "great plan of happiness," "the plan of redemption," and the "plan of salvation" (Alma 42:8, 11, 5), that plan—revealed in the Restoration—began with a Council in Heaven. As spirits, we desired to achieve the eternal life enjoyed by our heavenly parents. At that point we had progressed as far as we could without a mortal experience in a physical body. To provide that experience, God the Father planned to create this earth. In the planned mortal life, we would be soiled by sin as we faced the opposition necessary for our spiritual growth. We would also become subject to physical death. To reclaim us from death and sin, our Heavenly Father's plan would provide a Savior. His Resurrection would redeem all from death, and His atoning sacrifice would pay the price necessary for all to be cleansed from sin on the conditions prescribed to promote our growth. This Atonement of Jesus Christ is central to the Father's plan.

In the Council in Heaven, all the spirit children of God were introduced to the Father's plan, including its mortal consequences and trials, its heavenly helps, and its glorious destiny. We saw the end from the beginning. All of the myriads of mortals who have been born on this earth chose the Father's plan and fought for it in the heavenly contest that followed. Many also made covenants with the Father concerning what they would do in mortality. In ways that have not been revealed, our actions in the spirit world have influenced our circumstances in mortality.

Mortality and Spirit World

I will now summarize some of the principal elements of the Father's plan as they affect us during our mortal journeys and in the spirit world that follows.

The purpose of mortal life and the postmortal growth that can follow it is for the offspring of God to become like He is. This is Heavenly Father's desire for all His children. To achieve this joyful destiny, eternal laws require that we must become purified beings through the Atonement of Jesus Christ so we can dwell in the presence of the Father and the Son and enjoy the blessings of exaltation. As the Book of Mormon teaches, He invites "all to come unto him and partake of his goodness; and he denieth none that come unto him, black and white, bond and free, male and female; and he remembereth the heathen; and all are alike unto God" (2 Nephi 26:33; see also Alma 5:49).

The divine plan for us to become what we are destined to become requires us to make choices to reject the evil opposition that tempts mortals to act contrary to God's commandments and His plan. It also requires that we be subject to other mortal opposition, such as from the sins of others or from some defects of birth. Sometimes our needed growth is achieved better by suffering and adversity than by comfort and tranquility. And none of this mortal opposition could achieve its eternal purpose if divine intervention relieved us from all the adverse consequences of mortality.

The plan reveals our destiny in eternity, the purpose and conditions of our journey in mortality, and the heavenly helps we will receive. The commandments of God warn us against straying into dangerous circumstances. The teachings of inspired leaders guide our path and give assurances that promote our eternal journey.

God's plan gives us four great assurances to assist our journey through mortality. All are given to us through the Atonement of Jesus Christ, the centerpiece of the plan. The *first* assures us that through His suffering for the sins of which we repent, we can be cleansed of those sins. Then the merciful final judge will "remember them no more" (Doctrine and Covenants 58:42).

Second, as part of our Savior's Atonement, He took upon Him all other mortal infirmities. This allows us to receive divine help and strength to bear the inevitable burdens of mortality, personal and general, such as war and pestilence. The Book of Mormon provides our clearest scriptural description of this essential power of the Atonement. The Savior took upon Him "the pains and the sicknesses [and infirmities] of his people. . . . He will take upon him their infirmities, that his bowels may be filled with mercy, according to the flesh, that he may know according to the flesh how to succor his people according to their infirmities" (Alma 7:11–12).

Third, the Savior, through His infinite Atonement, revokes the finality of death and gives us the joyful assurance that all of us will be resurrected. The Book of Mormon teaches, "This restoration shall come to all, both old and young, both bond and free, both male and female, both the wicked and the righteous; and even there shall not so much as a hair of their heads be lost; but every thing shall be restored to its perfect frame" (Alma 11:44).

We celebrate the reality of the Resurrection in this Easter season. This gives us the perspective and strength to endure the mortal challenges faced by each of us and those we love, such things as the physical, mental, or emotional deficiencies we acquire at birth or experience during our mortal lives. Because of the Resurrection, we know that these mortal deficiencies are only temporary!

The restored gospel assures us that the Resurrection can include the opportunity to be with our family members—husband, wife, children, and parents. This is a powerful encouragement for us to fulfill our family responsibilities in mortality. It helps us live together in love in this life in anticipation of joyful reunions and associations in the next.

Fourth and finally, modern revelation teaches us that our progress need not conclude with the end of mortality. Little has been revealed about this important assurance. We are told that this life is the time to prepare to meet God and that we should not procrastinate our repentance (see Alma 34:32–33). Still, we are taught that in the spirit world the gospel is preached even to "the wicked and the disobedient who had rejected the truth" (Doctrine and Covenants 138:29) and that those taught there are capable of repentance in advance of the Final Judgment (see verses 31–34, 57–59).

Here are some other fundamentals of our Heavenly Father's plan:

The restored gospel of Jesus Christ gives us a unique perspective on the subjects of chastity, marriage, and the bearing of children. It teaches that marriage according to God's plan is necessary for accomplishing the purpose of God's plan, to provide the divinely appointed setting for mortal birth, and to prepare family members for eternal life. "Marriage is ordained of God unto man," the Lord said, " . . . that the earth might answer the end of its creation" (Doctrine and Covenants 49:15–16). In this, His plan, of course, runs counter to some strong worldly forces in law and custom.

The power to create mortal life is the most exalted power God has given His children. Its use was mandated in the first commandment to Adam and Eve, but another important commandment was given to forbid its misuse. Outside the bonds of marriage, all uses of the procreative power are to one degree or another a sinful degrading and perversion of the most divine attribute of men and women. The emphasis the restored gospel places on this law of chastity is because of the purpose of our procreative powers in the accomplishment of God's plan.

What Next?

During this 200th anniversary of the First Vision, which initiated the Restoration, we know the Lord's plan and we are encouraged by two centuries of its blessings through His restored Church. In this year of 2020, we have what is popularly called 20/20 vision for the events of the past.

As we look to the future, however, our vision is far less sure. We know that two centuries after the Restoration, the spirit world now includes many mortally experienced workers to accomplish the preaching that occurs there. We also know that we now have many more temples to perform the ordinances of eternity for those who repent and embrace the Lord's gospel on either side of the veil of death. All of this furthers our Heavenly Father's plan. God's love is so great that, except for the few who deliberately become sons of perdition, He has provided a destiny of glory for all of His children (see Doctrine and Covenants 76:43).

We know that the Savior will return and that there will be a millennium of peaceful reign to wrap up the mortal part of God's plan. We also know that there will be different resurrections, of the just and the unjust, with the final judgment of each person always following his or her resurrection.

We will be judged according to our actions, the desires of our hearts, and the kind of person we have become. This judgment will cause all of the children of God to proceed to a kingdom of glory for which their obedience has qualified them and where they will be comfortable. The judge of all this is our Savior, Jesus Christ (see John 5:22; 2 Nephi 9:41). His omniscience gives Him a perfect knowledge of all of our acts and desires, both those unrepented or unchanged and those repented or righteous. Therefore, after His judgment we will all confess "that his judgments are just" (Mosiah 16:1).

In conclusion, I share the conviction that has come to me from many letters and by reviewing many requests to return to the Church after name removal or apostasy. Many of our members do not fully understand this plan of salvation, which answers most questions about the doctrine and inspired policies of the restored Church. We who know God's plan and who have covenanted to participate have a clear responsibility to teach these truths and do all that we can to further them for others and in our own circumstances in mortality. I testify of Jesus Christ, our Savior and Redeemer, who makes it all possible, in the name of Jesus Christ, amen.

Note

1. "The Restoration of the Fulness of the Gospel of Jesus Christ: A Bicentennial Proclamation to the World," in Russell M. Nelson, "Hear Him," *Ensign* or *Liahona*, May 2020, 91.

THE BLESSING OF CONTINUING REVELATION TO PROPHETS AND PERSONAL REVELATION TO GUIDE OUR LIVES

ELDER QUENTIN L. COOK
Of the Quorum of the Twelve Apostles

Today I will speak on continuing revelation to prophets and continuing personal revelation to guide our lives.

Sometimes we receive revelation even when we do not know the Lord's purposes. Shortly before Elder Jeffrey R. Holland was called to be an Apostle in June of 1994, I had a beautiful revelatory experience that he would be called. I was a regional representative and could see no reason I would be given that knowledge. But we were companions as young missionaries in England in the early 1960s, and I had a great love for him. I considered the experience a tender mercy for me. In recent years, I have wondered if the Lord was preparing me to be junior in the Twelve to an incredible missionary companion who was my junior companion when we were young missionaries.[1] I sometimes warn young missionaries to be kind to their junior companions because they never know when they might be their senior companion.

I have a firm testimony that this restored Church is led by our Savior, Jesus Christ. He knows whom to call as His Apostles and in what order to call them. He also knows how to prepare His senior Apostle to be the prophet and President of the Church.

We were blessed this morning to hear our beloved prophet, President Russell M. Nelson, deliver a profound bicentennial proclamation to the world with respect to the Restoration of the fulness of the gospel of Jesus Christ.[2] This seminal declaration by President Nelson has made it clear that the Church of Jesus Christ owes its origin, existence, and direction for the future to the principle of continuous revelation. The new proclamation represents a loving Father's communication to His children.

In an earlier day, President Spencer W. Kimball expressed the feelings I have today. He stated: "Of all things, that . . . we should be most grateful [for] is that the heavens are indeed open and that the restored church of Jesus Christ is founded upon the rock of revelation. Continuous revelation is indeed the very lifeblood of the gospel of the living Lord and Savior, Jesus Christ."[3]

The prophet Enoch foresaw the days in which we live. The Lord acknowledged to Enoch the great wickedness that would prevail and prophesied of the "great tribulations" that would occur. Nevertheless, the Lord promised, "But my people will I preserve."[4] "And righteousness will I send down out of heaven; and truth will I send forth out of the earth, to bear testimony of mine Only Begotten."[5]

President Ezra Taft Benson taught with great power that the Book of Mormon, the keystone of our religion, came forth out of the earth in fulfillment of the Lord's pronouncement to Enoch. The Father and the Son and angels and prophets appearing to the Prophet Joseph Smith were "directed by heaven to restore the necessary powers to the kingdom."[6]

The Prophet Joseph Smith received revelation after revelation. Some have been addressed during this conference. Many revelations received by the Prophet Joseph have been preserved for us in the Doctrine and Covenants. All the standard works of the Church contain the mind and will of the Lord for us in this last dispensation.[7]

In addition to these great foundational scriptures, we are blessed with continuing revelation to living prophets. Prophets are "commissioned agents of the Lord, authorized to speak for Him."[8]

Some revelations are of monumental importance, and others enhance our understanding of essential divine truths and provide guidance for our day.[9]

We are incredibly grateful for the revelation to President Spencer W. Kimball extending priesthood and temple blessings to all worthy male members of the Church in June 1978.[10]

I have served with many of the Twelve who were present and participated when that precious revelation was received. Each of them, in personal conversations, confirmed the powerful and uniting spiritual guidance President Kimball and they had experienced.

Many said it was the most powerful revelation they had received before or after that time.[11]

Those of us currently serving in the Quorum of the Twelve Apostles have been blessed in our day as significant revelations have come through recent prophets.[12] President Russell M. Nelson has been a commissioned agent of the Lord *especially* with respect to revelations to help families build sanctuaries of faith in their homes, gather scattered Israel on both sides of the veil, and bless endowed members in sacred temple ordinance matters.

When important changes to bless our homes were announced at the October 2018 general conference, I testified "that in the deliberations of the Council of the First Presidency and Quorum of the Twelve Apostles in the temple, . . . after our beloved prophet petitioned the Lord for revelation . . . , a powerful confirmation was received by all."[13]

At that time, other revelations relating to sacred temple ordinances had been received but not announced or implemented.[14] This guidance commenced with individual prophetic revelation to President Russell M. Nelson and tender and powerful confirmation to those participating in the process. President Nelson specifically involved the sisters who preside over the Relief Society, Young Women, and Primary organizations. The final guidance, in the temple, to the First Presidency and Quorum of the Twelve Apostles was profoundly spiritual and powerful. We each knew we had received the mind, will, and voice of the Lord.[15]

I declare with all solemnity that continuous revelation has been received and is being received through channels the Lord has established. I testify the new proclamation President Nelson delivered this morning is a revelation to bless all people.

We Extend an Invitation to All to Feast at the Lord's Table

We also declare our heartfelt desire to be reunited with those who have been struggling with their testimonies, been less active, or had their names removed from Church records. We desire to feast with you "upon the words of Christ" at the Lord's table, to learn the things we all should do.[16] We need you! The Church needs you! The Lord needs you! Our heartfelt prayer is that you will join with us in worshipping the Savior of the world. We know that some of you may have received offense, unkindness, or other conduct that is not Christlike. We also know that some have had challenges to their faith that may not be fully appreciated, understood, or resolved.

Some of our most stalwart and faithful members have suffered a challenge to their faith for a season. I love the true account of W. W. Phelps, who had forsaken the Church and testified against the Prophet Joseph Smith in a Missouri court. After repenting, he wrote to Joseph, "I know my situation, you know it, and God knows it, and I want to be saved if my friends will help me."[17] Joseph did forgive him, put him back to work, and lovingly wrote, "Friends at first are friends again at last."[18]

Brothers and sisters, regardless of your situation, please know that the Church and its members will welcome you back!

Personal Revelation to Guide Our Lives

Personal revelation is available to all those who humbly seek guidance from the Lord. It is as important as prophetic revelation. Personal, spiritual revelation from the Holy Ghost has resulted in millions receiving the testimony necessary to be baptized and confirmed members of The Church of Jesus Christ of Latter-day Saints.

Personal revelation is the profound blessing received following baptism when we are "sanctified by the reception of the Holy Ghost."[19] I can remember a special spiritual revelation when I was 15 years old. My precious brother was seeking guidance from the Lord as to how to respond to our dear father, who did not want my brother to serve a mission. I prayed with sincere intent too and received personal revelation of the truthfulness of the gospel.

The Role of the Holy Ghost

Personal revelation is based on spiritual truths received from the Holy Ghost.[20] The Holy Ghost is the revealer and testifier of all truth, especially that of the Savior. Without the Holy Ghost, we could not really know that Jesus is the Christ. His seminal role is to bear witness of the Father and the Son and Their titles and Their glory.

The Holy Ghost can influence everyone in a powerful way.[21] This influence will not be constant unless one is baptized and receives the gift of the Holy Ghost. The Holy Ghost serves also as a cleansing agent in the process of repentance and forgiveness.

The Spirit communicates in marvelous ways. The Lord used this beautiful description:

"I will tell you in your mind and in your heart, by the Holy Ghost, which shall come upon you and which shall dwell in your heart.

"Now, behold, this is the spirit of revelation."[22]

Although its impact can be incredibly powerful, it most often comes quietly as a still, small voice.[23] The scriptures include many examples of how the Spirit influences our minds, including speaking peace to our minds,[24] occupying our minds,[25] enlightening our minds,[26] and even sending a voice to our minds.[27]

Some principles that prepare us to receive revelation include:

Praying for spiritual guidance. Reverently and humbly we need to seek and ask[28] and be patient and submissive.[29]

Preparing for inspiration. This requires that we be in harmony with the Lord's teachings and in compliance with His commandments.

Partaking of the sacrament worthily. When we do this, we witness and covenant with God that we take upon ourselves the name of His holy Son and that we remember Him and keep His commandments.

These principles prepare us to receive, recognize, and follow the prompting and guidance of the Holy Ghost. This includes the "peaceable things . . . which bringeth joy [and] . . . life eternal."[30]

Our spiritual preparation is greatly enhanced when we regularly study the scriptures and truths of the gospel and ponder in our minds the guidance we seek. But remember to be patient and trust in the Lord's timing. Guidance is given by an omniscient Lord when He "deliberately chooses to school us."[31]

Revelation in Our Callings and Assignments

The Holy Ghost will also provide revelation in our callings and assignments. In my experience, significant spiritual guidance most often comes when we are trying to bless others in fulfilling our responsibilities.

I can remember as a young bishop receiving a desperate call from a married couple a short time before I was to catch an airplane for a business engagement. I pled with the Lord before their arrival to know how I could bless them. It was revealed to me the nature of the problem and the response I should give. That revelatory guidance allowed me to fulfill the sacred responsibilities of my calling as bishop despite very limited availability of time. Bishops all over the world also share these same kinds of experiences with me. As a stake president, I not only received important revelation but also received personal *correction* that was necessary to accomplish the Lord's purposes.

I assure you that revelatory guidance can be received by each of us as we humbly labor in the Lord's vineyard. Most of our guidance comes from the Holy Ghost. Sometimes and for some purposes, it comes directly from the Lord. I personally testify that this is true. Guidance for the Church, as a whole, comes to the President and prophet of the Church.

We, as modern Apostles, have had the privilege of working and traveling with our current prophet, President Nelson. I paraphrase what Wilford Woodruff said about the Prophet Joseph Smith; it is equally true of President Nelson. I have seen "the workings of the Spirit of God with him, and the revelations of Jesus Christ unto him and the fulfillment of those revelations."[32]

My humble plea today is that each of us will seek continuing revelation to guide our lives and follow the Spirit as we worship God the Father in the name of our Savior, Jesus Christ, of whom I bear witness in the name of Jesus Christ, amen.

Notes

1. In 1960 when the age for missionary service for young men was reduced from 20 to 19 years of age, I was one of the last 20-year-olds; Elder Jeffrey R. Holland was one of the first 19-year-olds.

2. See "The Restoration of the Fulness of the Gospel of Jesus Christ: A Bicentennial Proclamation to the World," in Russell M. Nelson, "Hear Him," *Ensign* or *Liahona*, May 2020, 91. This proclamation joins with five others that have been delivered in this dispensation by the First Presidency and the Quorum of the Twelve Apostles.
3. *Teachings of Presidents of the Church: Spencer W. Kimball* (2006), 243; see also Matthew 16:13–19.
4. Moses 7:61.
5. Moses 7:62. The Lord continued, "And righteousness and truth will I cause to sweep the earth as with a flood, to gather out mine elect from the four quarters of the earth" (Moses 7:62; see also Psalm 85:11).
6. Ezra Taft Benson, "The Gift of Modern Revelation," *Ensign,* Nov. 1986, 80.
7. See Ezra Taft Benson, "The Gift of Modern Revelation," 80.
8. Hugh B. Brown, "Joseph Smith among the Prophets" (Sixteenth Annual Joseph Smith Memorial Sermon, Logan Institute of Religion, Dec. 7, 1958), 7.
9. See Hugh B. Brown, "Joseph Smith among the Prophets," 7. In all cases, the revelations are in harmony with the word of God given to previous prophets.
10. See Official Declaration 2; see also 2 Nephi 26:33. The revelation implemented doctrine set forth in the Book of Mormon that "all are alike unto God," including "black and white, bond and free, male and female" (2 Nephi 26:33). This remarkable revelation was received and confirmed in the sacred upper room of the Salt Lake Temple by the Council of the First Presidency and Quorum of the Twelve Apostles.
11. Many of the Apostles indicated that the revelation was so powerful and so sacred that any words used to describe it would be insufficient and, in some ways, would diminish the deep and powerful nature of the revelation.
12. See "The Family: A Proclamation to the World," *Ensign* or *Liahona,* May 2017, 145. This proclamation was announced by President Gordon B. Hinckley at the general Relief Society meeting held on September 23, 1995, in Salt Lake City, Utah. See also Thomas S. Monson, "Welcome to Conference," *Ensign* or *Liahona,* Nov. 2012, 4–5. President Monson announced a lower age requirement for missionary service.
13. Quentin L. Cook, "Deep and Lasting Conversion to Heavenly Father and the Lord Jesus Christ," *Ensign* or *Liahona,* Nov. 2018, 11.
14. The revelations related to sacred temple ordinances were implemented in all temples beginning on January 1, 2019. It is important to understand that specific details about temple ordinances are discussed only in the temple. However, principles are taught. Elder David A. Bednar beautifully taught the significance of temple covenants and ordinances and how through them "the power of godliness can flow into our lives" ("Let This House Be Built unto My Name," *Ensign* or *Liahona,* May 2020, 86).
15. This process and the meetings held occurred in the Salt Lake Temple in January, February, March, and April 2018. The final revelation to the First Presidency and the Quorum of the Twelve was on April 26, 2018.
16. See 2 Nephi 32:3.
17. *Saints: The Story of the Church of Jesus Christ in the Latter Days,* vol. 1, *The Standard of Truth, 1815–1846* (2018), 418.
18. *Saints,* 1:418.
19. 3 Nephi 27:20.
20. The Holy Ghost is a member of the Godhead (see 1 John 5:7; Doctrine and Covenants 20:28). He has a body of spirit in the form and likeness of man (see Doctrine and Covenants 130:22). His influence can be everywhere. He is unified in purpose with our Heavenly Father and Jesus Christ, our Savior.
21. For a comprehensive understanding of the Light of Christ and the difference between the Light of Christ and the Holy Ghost, see 2 Nephi 32; Doctrine and Covenants 88:7, 11–13; "Light of Christ," Bible Dictionary. See also Boyd K. Packer, "The Light of Christ," *Ensign* or *Liahona,* Apr. 2005, 8–14.
22. Doctrine and Covenants 8:2–3.
23. See Helaman 5:30; Doctrine and Covenants 85:6.
24. See Doctrine and Covenants 6:23.
25. See Doctrine and Covenants 128:1.

SUNDAY AFTERNOON SESSION

26. See Doctrine and Covenants 11:13.
27. See Enos 1:10.
28. See Matthew 7:7–8.
29. See Mosiah 3:19.
30. Doctrine and Covenants 42:61.
31. Neal A. Maxwell, *All These Things Shall Give Thee Experience* (2007), 31.
32. Wilford Woodruff, in *Teachings of Presidents of the Church: Joseph Smith* (2007), 283.

FINDING REFUGE FROM THE STORMS OF LIFE

ELDER RICARDO P. GIMÉNEZ

Of the Seventy

Back in the mid-90s, during my college years, I was part of the Fourth Company of the Santiago Fire Department in Chile. While serving there, I lived at the fire station as part of the night guard. Toward the end of the year, I was told that I had to be at the fire station on New Year's Eve because on that day there was almost always some emergency. Surprised, I replied, "Really?"

Well, I remember waiting with my associates when, at midnight, fireworks began shooting off in downtown Santiago. We started hugging each other with well wishes for the new year. Suddenly the bells at the fire station began ringing, indicating that there was an emergency. We got our equipment and jumped on the fire engine. On our way to the emergency, as we passed crowds of people celebrating the new year, I noticed that they were largely unconcerned and carefree. They were relaxed and enjoying the warm summer night. Yet somewhere nearby, the people we were hurrying to help were in serious trouble.

This experience helped me realize that although our lives may at times be relatively smooth, the time will come for each of us when we will face unexpected challenges and storms that will push the limits of our ability to endure. Physical, mental, family, and employment challenges; natural disasters; and other matters of life or death are but some of the examples of the storms that we will face in this life.

When faced with these storms, we often experience feelings of despair or fear. President Russell M. Nelson said, "Faith is the antidote for fear"—*faith in our Lord Jesus Christ* ("Let Your Faith Show," *Ensign* or *Liahona,* May 2014, 29). As I have seen the storms that affect people's lives, I have concluded that no matter what kind of storm is battering us—regardless of whether there is a solution to it or whether there is an end in sight—there is only one refuge, and it is the same for all types of storms. This single refuge provided by our Heavenly Father is our Lord Jesus Christ and His Atonement.

None of us are exempt from facing these storms. Helaman, a Book of Mormon prophet, taught us as follows: "Remember that it is upon the rock of our Redeemer, who is Christ, the Son of God, that ye must build your foundation; that when the devil shall send forth his mighty winds, yea, his shafts in the whirlwind, yea, when all his hail and his mighty storm shall beat upon you, it shall have no power over you to drag you down to the gulf of misery and endless wo, because of the rock upon which ye are built, which is a sure foundation, a foundation whereon if men build they cannot fall" (Helaman 5:12).

Elder Robert D. Hales, who had his own experiences with enduring storms, said: "Suffering is universal; how we react to suffering is individual. Suffering can take us one of two ways. It can be a strengthening and purifying experience combined with faith, or it can be a destructive force in our lives if we do not have the faith in the Lord's atoning sacrifice" ("Your Sorrow Shall Be Turned to Joy," *Ensign,* Nov. 1983, 66).

In order to enjoy the refuge that Jesus Christ and His Atonement offer, we must have faith in Him—a faith that will allow us to rise above all the pains of a limited, earthly perspective. He has promised that He will make our burdens light if we come unto Him in all that we do.

"Come unto me," He said, "all ye that labour and are heavy laden, and I will give you rest.

"Take my yoke upon you, and learn of me; for I am meek and lowly in heart: and ye shall find rest unto your souls.

"For my yoke is easy, and my burden is light" (Matthew 11:28–30; see also Mosiah 24:14–15).

It is said that "to one who has faith, no explanation is necessary. To one without faith, no explanation is possible." (This statement has been attributed to Thomas Aquinas but is most likely a loose paraphrase of things he taught.) However, we have limited understanding of the things that happen here on earth, and often we do not have answers to the question of *why*. Why is this happening? Why is this happening to *me*? What am I supposed to learn? When answers evade us, that is when the words expressed by our Savior to the Prophet Joseph Smith in Liberty Jail are completely applicable:

"My son, peace be unto thy soul; thine adversity and thine afflictions shall be but a small moment;

"And then, if thou endure it well, God shall exalt thee on high" (Doctrine and Covenants 121:7–8).

Although many people indeed believe *in* Jesus Christ, the key question is whether we *believe* Him and whether we *believe* the things that He teaches us and asks us to do. Perhaps someone might think, "What does Jesus Christ know about what is happening to me? How does He know what I need to be happy?" Truly, it was our Redeemer and Intercessor to whom the prophet Isaiah was referring when he said:

"He is despised and rejected of men; a man of sorrows, and acquainted with grief. . . .

"Surely he hath borne our griefs, and carried our sorrows. . . .

"But he was wounded for our transgressions, he was bruised for our iniquities: the chastisement of our peace was upon him; and with his stripes we are healed" (Isaiah 53:3–5).

The Apostle Peter also taught us about the Savior, saying, "Who his own self bare our sins in his own body on the tree, that we, being dead to sins, should live unto righteousness: by whose stripes ye were healed" (1 Peter 2:24).

Although the time of Peter's own martyrdom was approaching, his words are not filled with fear or pessimism; rather, he taught the Saints to "rejoice," even though they were "in heaviness through manifold temptations." Peter counseled us to remember that "the trial of [our] faith, . . . though it be tried with fire," would lead to "praise and honour and glory at the appearing of Jesus Christ" and to "the salvation of [our] souls" (1 Peter 1:6–7, 9).

Peter continued:

"Beloved, think it not strange concerning the fiery trial which is to try you, as though some strange thing happened unto you:

"But rejoice, inasmuch as ye are partakers of Christ's sufferings; that, when his glory shall be revealed, ye may be glad also with exceeding joy" (1 Peter 4:12–13).

President Russell M. Nelson taught that "Saints can be happy under every circumstance. . . . When the focus of our lives is on God's plan of salvation . . . and Jesus Christ and His gospel, we can feel joy regardless of what is happening—or not happening—in our lives. Joy comes from and because of Him. He is the source of all joy" ("Joy and Spiritual Survival," *Ensign* or *Liahona,* Nov. 2016, 82).

Of course, it is easier to say these things when we are not in the midst of a storm than to live and apply them during the storm. But as your brother, I hope you can feel that I sincerely want to share with you how valuable it is to know that Jesus Christ and His Atonement are the refuge that we all need, regardless of the storms that are battering our lives.

I know that we are all children of God, that He loves us, and that we are not alone. I invite you to come and see that He can lighten your burdens and be the refuge you are seeking. Come and help others find the refuge that they so yearn for. Come and stay with us in this refuge, which will help you resist the storms of life. There is no doubt in my heart that if you come, you will see, you will help, and you will stay.

The prophet Alma testified the following to his son Helaman: "I do know that whosoever shall put their trust in God shall be supported in their trials, and their troubles, and their afflictions, and shall be lifted up at the last day" (Alma 36:3).

The Savior Himself said:

"Let your hearts be comforted . . . ; for all flesh is in mine hands; be still and know that I am God. . . .

"Wherefore, fear not even unto death; for in this world your joy is not full, but in me your joy is full" (Doctrine and Covenants 101:16, 36).

The hymn "Be Still, My Soul," which has touched my heart on many occasions, has a message of comfort for our souls. The lyrics read as follows:

Be still, my soul: The hour is hast'ning on
When we shall be forever with the Lord,

> *When disappointment, grief, and fear are gone,*
> *Sorrow forgot, love's purest joys restored.*
> *Be still, my soul: When change and tears are past,*
> *All safe and blessed we shall meet at last.*
> (*Hymns*, no. 124)

As we face the storms of life, I know that if we make our best effort and rely upon Jesus Christ and His Atonement as our refuge, we will be blessed with the relief, comfort, strength, temperance, and peace that we are seeking, with certainty in our hearts that at the end of our time here on earth, we will hear the words of the Master: "Well done, thou good and faithful servant: . . . enter thou into the joy of thy lord" (Matthew 25:21). In the name of Jesus Christ, amen.

COME AND BELONG

ELDER DIETER F. UCHTDORF
Of the Quorum of the Twelve Apostles

My dear brothers and sisters, my dear friends, each week members of The Church of Jesus Christ of Latter-day Saints all around the globe worship our beloved Heavenly Father, the God and King of the universe, and His Beloved Son, Jesus Christ. We ponder the life and teachings of Jesus Christ—the only sinless soul who ever lived, the spotless Lamb of God. As often as we can, we partake of the sacrament in remembrance of His sacrifice and recognize that He is the center in our lives.

We love Him and we honor Him. Because of His profound and eternal love, Jesus Christ suffered and died for you and me. He broke open the gates of death, shattered the barriers that separated friends and loved ones,[1] and brought hope to the hopeless, healing to the sick, and deliverance to the captive.[2]

To Him we dedicate our hearts, our lives, and our daily devotion. For this reason, "we talk of Christ, we rejoice in Christ, [and] we preach of Christ, . . . that our children may know to what source they may look for a remission of their sins."[3]

Practicing Discipleship

However, being a disciple of Jesus Christ involves much more than talking and preaching of Christ. The Savior Himself restored His Church to help us on the path to become more like Him. The Church of Jesus Christ of Latter-day Saints is structured to provide opportunities to practice the fundamentals of discipleship. Through our participation in the Church, we learn to recognize and act on the promptings of the Holy Spirit. We develop the disposition of reaching out in compassion and kindness to others.

This is an effort of a lifetime, and it requires practice.

Accomplished athletes spend countless hours practicing the fundamentals of their sports. Nurses, networkers, nuclear engineers, and even I as a competitive hobby cook in Harriet's kitchen become capable and skilled only as we diligently practice our craft.

As an airline captain, I often trained pilots using a flight simulator—a sophisticated machine that replicates the flying experience. The simulator not only helps pilots learn the fundamentals of flying; it also allows them to experience and react to unexpected events they could encounter when they take command of the real aircraft.

The same principles apply for disciples of Jesus Christ.

Actively participating in the Church of Jesus Christ and its great variety of opportunities will help us to be better prepared for life's changing circumstances, whatever and however serious they may be. As members of the Church, we are encouraged to immerse ourselves in the words of God through His prophets, ancient and modern. Through sincere and humble prayer to our Heavenly Father, we learn to recognize the voice of the Holy Spirit. We accept calls to serve, teach, plan, minister, and administer. These opportunities allow us to grow in spirit, mind, and character.

They will help us prepare to make and keep sacred covenants that will bless us in this life and in the life to come.

Come, Join with Us!

We invite all of God's children throughout the world to join us in this great endeavor. Come and see! Even during this challenging time of COVID-19, meet with us online. Meet with our missionaries online. Find out for yourself what this Church is all about! When this difficult time has passed, meet with us in our homes and in our worship places!

We invite you to come and help! Come and serve with us, ministering to God's children, following in the footsteps of the Savior, and making this world a better place.

Come and belong! You will make us stronger. And you will become better, kinder, and happier as well. Your faith will deepen and grow more resilient—more capable of withstanding the turbulences and unexpected trials of life.

And how do we start? There are many possible ways.

We invite you to read the Book of Mormon. If you don't have a copy, you can read it on ChurchofJesusChrist.org[4] or download the Book of Mormon app. The Book of Mormon is another testament of Jesus Christ and a companion to the Old and New Testaments. We love all of these holy scriptures and learn from them.

We invite you to spend some time at ComeuntoChrist.org to find out what members of the Church teach and believe.

Invite the missionaries to visit with you online or in the privacy of your home where this is possible—they have a message of hope and healing. These missionaries are our precious sons and daughters who serve in many places around the world on their own time and money.

In the Church of Jesus Christ, you will find a family of people who are not so different from you. You will find people who need your help and who want to help you as you strive to become the best version of yourself—the person God created you to become.

The Savior's Embrace Extends to All

You might be thinking, "I have made mistakes in my life. I'm not sure I could ever feel like I belong in the Church of Jesus Christ. God couldn't be interested in someone like me."

Jesus the Christ, though He is "the King of kings,"[5] the Messiah, "the Son of the living God,"[6] does care deeply about each and every one of God's children. He cares regardless of a person's position—how poor or rich, how imperfect or proven someone is. During His mortal life, the Savior ministered to all: to the happy and accomplished, to the broken and lost, and to those without hope. Often, the people He served and ministered to were not individuals of prominence, beauty, or wealth. Often, the people He lifted up had little to offer in return but gratitude, a humble heart, and the desire to have faith.

If Jesus spent His mortal life ministering to "the least of these,"[7] would He not love them today? Is there not a place in His Church for all of God's children? Even for those who feel unworthy, forgotten, or alone?

There is no threshold of perfection you must attain in order to qualify for God's grace. Your prayers do not have to be loud or eloquent or grammatically correct in order to reach heaven.

In truth, God does not show favoritism[8]—the things the world values mean nothing to Him. He knows your heart, and He loves you regardless of your title, financial net worth, or number of Instagram followers.

As we incline our hearts to our Heavenly Father and draw near to Him, we will feel Him draw near to us.[9]

We are His beloved children.

Even those who reject Him.

Even those who, like a headstrong, unruly child, become angry with God and His Church, pack their bags, and storm out the door proclaiming that they're running away and never coming back.

When a child runs away from home, he or she may not notice the concerned parents looking out the window. With tender hearts, they watch their son or daughter go—hoping their precious child will learn something from this heartrending experience and perhaps see life with new eyes—and eventually return home.

So it is with our loving Heavenly Father. He is waiting for our return.

Your Savior, tears of love and compassion in His eyes, awaits your return. Even when you feel far away from God, He will see you; He will have compassion for you and run to embrace you.[10]

Come and belong.

God Allows Us to Learn from Our Mistakes

We are pilgrims walking the road of mortality in a grand search for meaning and ultimate truth. Often, all we see is the path directly ahead—we cannot see where the bends in the road will lead. Our loving Heavenly Father has not given us every answer. He expects us to figure out many things for ourselves. He expects us to believe—even when it's difficult to do so.

He expects us to straighten our shoulders and develop a little resolve—a little backbone—and take another step forward.

That is the way we learn and grow.

Would you honestly want everything spelled out in every detail? Would you honestly want every question answered? Every destination mapped out?

I believe most of us would tire very quickly of this sort of heavenly micromanagement. We learn the important lessons of life through experience. Through learning from our mistakes. Through repenting and realizing for ourselves that "wickedness never was happiness."[11]

Jesus Christ, the Son of God, died so that our mistakes might not condemn us and forever halt our progress. Because of Him, we can repent, and our mistakes can become stepping-stones to greater glory.

You don't have to walk this road alone. Our Heavenly Father has not left us to wander in darkness.

This is why, in the spring of 1820, He appeared with His Son, Jesus Christ, to a young man, Joseph Smith.

Think of that for a moment! The God of the universe appeared to man!

This was the first of many encounters Joseph had with God and other heavenly beings. Many of the words these divine beings spoke to him are recorded in the scriptures of The Church of Jesus Christ of Latter-day Saints. They are easily accessible. Anyone can read them and learn for themselves the message God has for us in our day.

We invite you to study them for yourself.

Joseph Smith was quite young when he received these revelations. Most of them came before he was 30 years old.[12] He lacked experience, and to some people, he probably seemed underqualified to be the Lord's prophet.

And yet the Lord called him anyway—following a pattern we find throughout the holy scriptures.

God didn't wait to find a perfect person to restore His gospel.

If He had, He would still be waiting.

Joseph was a lot like you and me. Though Joseph made mistakes, God used him to accomplish His great purposes.

President Thomas S. Monson often repeated these words of advice: "Whom the Lord calls, the Lord qualifies."[13]

The Apostle Paul reasoned with the Saints in Corinth: "Consider your own call, brothers and sisters: not many of you were wise by human standards, not many were powerful, not many were of noble birth."[14]

God uses the weak and the plain to bring about His purposes. This truth stands as a testimony that it is God's power, not man's, that accomplishes His work on the earth.[15]

Hear Him, Follow Him

When God appeared to Joseph Smith, He introduced His Son, Jesus Christ, and said, "Hear Him!"[16]

Joseph spent the rest of his life hearing Him and following Him.

As with Joseph, our discipleship begins with our decision to hear and follow the Savior Jesus Christ.

If you desire to follow Him, gather your faith and take upon yourself His cross.

You will find that you *do* belong in His Church—a place of warmth and welcoming where you can join in the grand pursuit of discipleship and happiness.

It is my hope that, in this bicentennial year of the First Vision, as we contemplate and learn of the Restoration of the Church of Jesus Christ, we will realize that it is not just a historical event. You and I play a crucial part in this great, continuing story.

What, then, is your and my part?

It is to learn of Jesus Christ. To study His words. To hear Him and to follow Him by actively participating in this great work. I invite you to come and belong!

You don't have to be perfect. You only have to have a desire to develop your faith and draw nearer to Him each day.

Our part is to love and serve God and to love and serve God's children.

As you do so, God will encircle you with His love, joy, and certain guidance through this life, even under the most serious circumstances, and even beyond.

Of this I testify and leave you my blessing in deep gratitude and love for each one of you, in the sacred name of our Savior, our Master—in the name of Jesus Christ, amen.

Notes

1. See Ephesians 2:13–14.
2. See Luke 4:18.
3. 2 Nephi 25:26.
4. See the Book of Mormon at ChurchofJesusChrist.org/study/scriptures/bofm.
5. 1 Timothy 6:15.
6. See Matthew 16:15–17.
7. Matthew 25:40.
8. See Acts 10:34.
9. See Doctrine and Covenants 88:63.
10. See the reaction of the father who sees the return of his prodigal son in Luke 15:20.
11. Alma 41:10.
12. For example, of the 138 sections of the Doctrine and Covenants, more than 100 are revelations that Joseph Smith received before his 30th birthday, on December 23, 1835.
13. Thomas S. Monson, "Duty Calls," *Ensign,* May 1996, 44.
14. 1 Corinthians 1:26, New Revised Standard Version.
15. See 1 Corinthians 1:28–29; 2 Corinthians 4:7.
16. Joseph Smith—History 1:17.

THE FINEST HOMES

ELDER L. WHITNEY CLAYTON
Of the Presidency of the Seventy

Recently a billboard in Salt Lake City caught my eye. It advertised a furniture and interior design company. It stated simply, "Serving the Finest Homes in Salt Lake City."

The message was catchy—what is a "finest home"? I found myself thinking about that question, especially with regard to the children my wife, Kathy, and I raised and the children they are raising today. Like parents everywhere, we worried about and prayed over our family. We still do. We earnestly want the very best for them. How can they and their children live in the finest homes? I have reflected on the homes of Church members Kathy and I have been privileged to visit. We have been invited into homes in Korea and Kenya, in the Philippines and Peru, in Laos and Latvia. Let me share four observations about fine homes.

First, from the Lord's perspective, establishing the finest homes has everything to do with the personal qualities of the people who live there. These homes aren't made fine in any important or lasting way by their furniture or by the net worth or social status of the people who own them. The finest characteristic of any home is the image of Christ reflected in the home's residents. What matters is the interior design of the souls of the inhabitants, not the structure itself.

The attributes of Christ are acquired in the "process of time"[1] by intentional progress along the covenant path. Christlike attributes adorn the lives of those who strive to live with goodness. They fill homes with gospel light, whether the floor is mud or marble. Even if you are the only one in your household who follows the injunction to "seek after these things,"[2] you can contribute to the spiritual furnishings of your family's home.

We follow the Lord's counsel to "organize [ourselves]; prepare every needful thing; and establish a house" by organizing, preparing, and establishing our spiritual lives, not our real estate. As we patiently pursue the Savior's covenant path, our home becomes "a house of glory, a house of order, [and] a house of God."[3]

Second, residents in the finest homes make time to study the scriptures and the words of living prophets every day. President Russell M. Nelson has invited us to "transform" and "remodel" our homes through gospel study.[4] His invitation recognizes that fine homes house the tender, vital work of personal growth and remodeling our weaknesses. Daily repentance is a transformative tool that enables us to grow a little kinder, more loving, and more understanding. Studying the scriptures brings us closer to the Savior, whose generous love and grace assist us with our growth.

The Bible, Book of Mormon, and Pearl of Great Price tell the stories of families, so it's not surprising that those divine volumes are incomparable handbooks for constructing the finest homes. They chronicle the worries of parents, the perils of temptation, the triumph of righteousness, the trials of famine and abundance, and the horrors of war and rewards of peace. Again and again the scriptures show us how families succeed through righteous living and how they fail by pursuing other paths.

Third, fine homes follow the blueprint created by the Lord for His finest home, the temple. Building a temple begins with basic steps—clearing brush and leveling land. Those initial efforts to ready the ground might be compared to keeping the basic commandments. The commandments are the foundation on which discipleship is built. Steady discipleship leads us to become firm, steadfast, and immovable,[5] like the steel framework for a temple. This steady framework allows the Lord to send His Spirit to change our hearts.[6] Experiencing a mighty change of heart is like adding beautiful features to the interior of a temple.

As we continue in faith, the Lord gradually changes us. We receive His image in our countenance and begin to reflect the love and beauty of His character.[7] As we become more like Him, we will feel at home in His house, and He will feel at home in ours.

We can maintain our home's close connection to His home by qualifying for and using a temple recommend as frequently as circumstances allow. As we do so, the holiness of the Lord's house rests in our house as well.

The magnificent Salt Lake Temple stands nearby. Built by pioneers with rudimentary tools, local materials, and endless hard work, the temple was constructed from 1853 to 1893. The best the early Church members had to offer in engineering, architecture, and interior design created a masterpiece that is recognized by millions.

Nearly 130 years have passed since the temple was dedicated. As Elder Gary E. Stevenson noted yesterday, the engineering principles used to design the temple have been replaced by newer, safer standards. Failure to enhance the temple's engineering and repair structural weaknesses would betray the confidence of the pioneers, who did all they could and then left the temple's care to succeeding generations.

The Church has commenced a four-year restoration project to improve the temple's structural and seismic strength.[8] The foundation, floors, and walls will be fortified. The best engineering knowledge available today will bring the temple up to modern standards. We will not be able to see the structural changes, but their effects will be real and important. In all of this work, the temple's beautiful interior design features will be preserved.

We should follow the example being given to us by the Salt Lake Temple renovation and take time to evaluate our own spiritual seismic engineering to make sure it is up to date. Periodic self-assessment, coupled with asking the Lord, "What lack I yet?"[9] can help each of us contribute to the building of a finest home.

Fourth, the finest homes are refuges from the storms of life. The Lord has promised that those who keep the commandments of God "prosper in the land."[10] God's prosperity is the power to press forward despite the problems of life.

In 2002 I learned an important lesson about problems. While in Asunción, Paraguay, I met with the city's stake presidents. At that time, Paraguay faced a terrible financial crisis, and many Church members were suffering and unable to make ends meet. I had not been to South America since my mission and had never been to

Paraguay. I had been serving in that Area Presidency for only a few weeks. Apprehensive about my inability to give guidance to those stake presidents, I asked them to tell me only what was going well in their stakes. The first stake president told me about things that were going well. The next mentioned things that were going well and a few problems. By the time we got to the last stake president, he mentioned only a series of vexing challenges. As the stake presidents explained the magnitude of the situation, I grew increasingly concerned, nearly desperate, about what to say.

Just as the last stake president was finishing his comments, a thought came into my mind: "Elder Clayton, ask them this question: 'Presidents, of the members in your stakes who pay a full tithing, pay a generous fast offering, magnify their callings in the Church, actually visit their families as home teachers or visiting teachers[11] every month, hold family home evening, study the scriptures, and hold family prayer each day, how many have problems they cannot address on their own without the Church having to step in and solve their problems for them?'"

Responsive to the impression I had received, I asked the stake presidents that question.

They looked at me in surprised silence and then said, *"Pues, ninguno,"* meaning, "Well, no one." They then told me that none of the members who did all of those things had problems they were incapable of resolving on their own. Why? Because they lived in the finest homes. Their faithful living provided them the strength, vision, and heavenly help they needed in the economic turmoil that surrounded them.

This doesn't mean the righteous won't become ill, suffer accidents, face business reversals, or confront many other difficulties in life. Mortality always brings challenges, but time after time I have seen that those who strive to obey the commandments are blessed to find their way forward with peace and hope. Those blessings are available to everyone.[12]

David declared, "Except the Lord build the house, they labour in vain that build it."[13] Wherever you live, whatever your house looks like, and whatever the composition of your family, you can help build the finest home for your family. The restored gospel of Jesus Christ provides the plans for that home. The Savior is the perfect engineer, builder, and interior designer. His project is the perfection and eternal joy of our souls. With His loving help, your soul can be all He wants it to be and you can be the finest version of yourself, prepared to establish and live in a finest home.

I gratefully testify that the God and Father of us all lives. His Son, the Lord Jesus Christ, is the Savior and Redeemer of all mankind. They love us perfectly. The Church of Jesus Christ of Latter-day Saints is the Lord's kingdom on earth. Living prophets and apostles guide it today. The Book of Mormon is true. The restored gospel of Jesus Christ is the perfect blueprint for establishing finest homes. In the name of Jesus Christ, amen.

Notes

1. Moses 7:21.
2. Articles of Faith 1:13.
3. Doctrine and Covenants 88:119.
4. See Russell M. Nelson, "Becoming Exemplary Latter-day Saints," *Ensign* or *Liahona,* Nov. 2018, 113.
5. See 1 Nephi 2:10; Mosiah 5:15; 3 Nephi 6:14.
6. See Mosiah 5:2; Alma 5:7.
7. See Alma 5:14, 19.
8. An earthquake on March 18, 2020, amply demonstrated the need to undertake the project.
9. Matthew 19:20.
10. Mosiah 2:22.
11. Home teaching and visiting teaching were retired and ministering was implemented in 2018 (see Russell M. Nelson, "Ministering," *Ensign* or *Liahona,* May 2018, 100).
12. When we choose to not live in accordance with commandments, then the blessings of the Lord are withdrawn to some degree. This recurring pattern seen in the Book of Mormon is sometimes referred to as the cycle of righteousness and wickedness (see *Book of Mormon Student Manual* [Church Educational System manual, 2009], 414, ChurchofJesusChrist.org).
13. Psalm 127:1.

SHARING THE MESSAGE OF THE RESTORATION AND THE RESURRECTION

ELDER D. TODD CHRISTOFFERSON
Of the Quorum of the Twelve Apostles

Throughout this general conference we have spoken and sung with joy about the fulfillment of the long-ago prophesied "restitution of all things,"[1] about bringing "together in one all things in Christ,"[2] about the return of the fulness of the gospel, priesthood, and Church of Jesus Christ to the earth, all of which we capture in the title "the Restoration."

But the Restoration is not only for those of us who rejoice in it today. The revelations of the First Vision were not for Joseph Smith alone but are offered as light and truth for any who "lack wisdom."[3] The Book of Mormon is the possession of mankind. The priesthood ordinances of salvation and exaltation were prepared for every individual, including those who no longer dwell in mortality. The Church of Jesus Christ of Latter-day Saints and its blessings are intended for all who want them. The gift of the Holy Ghost is meant for everyone. The Restoration belongs to the world, and its message is especially urgent today.

"Wherefore, how great the importance to make these things known unto the inhabitants of the earth, that they may know that there is no flesh that can dwell in the presence of God, save it be through the merits, and mercy, and grace of the Holy Messiah, who layeth down his life according to the flesh, and taketh it again by the power of the Spirit, that he may bring to pass the resurrection of the dead."[4]

From the day that the Prophet's brother Samuel Smith filled his satchel with freshly printed copies of the Book of Mormon and set out on foot to share the new scripture, the Saints have labored without ceasing "to make these things known unto the inhabitants of the earth."

In 1920, then-Elder David O. McKay of the Quorum of the Twelve Apostles began a yearlong tour of the missions of the

Church. By May 1921, he was standing in a small cemetery in Fagaliʻi, Samoa, before the well-tended graves of three small children, the daughter and two sons of Thomas and Sarah Hilton. These little ones—the oldest was two—died during the time Thomas and Sarah served as a young missionary couple in the late 1800s.

Before he left Utah, Elder McKay promised Sarah, now a widow, that he would visit her children's graves in Samoa as she had never been able to return there. Elder McKay wrote back to her, "Your three little ones, Sister Hilton, in silence most eloquent . . . carry on your noble missionary work begun nearly thirty years ago." Then he added a verse of his own composition:

> *By loving hands their dying eyes were closed,*
> *By loving hands their little limbs composed,*
> *By foreign hands their humble graves adorned,*
> *By strangers honor'd, and by strangers mourned.*[5]

This story is but one of thousands, hundreds of thousands, that speak of the time, treasure, and lives sacrificed over the last 200 years to share the message of the Restoration. Our aspiration to reach every nation, kindred, tongue, and people is undiminished today, as witnessed by the tens of thousands of young men, women, and couples currently serving under full-time mission calls; by Church members generally, who echo Philip's invitation to come and see;[6] and by the millions of dollars spent annually to sustain this effort across the world.

While our invitations are without compulsion, we hope people will find them compelling. For that to be so, I believe at least three things are required: first, your love; second, your example; and third, your use of the Book of Mormon.

Our invitations cannot be a matter of self-interest; rather, they must be an expression of selfless love.[7] This love, known as charity, the pure love of Christ, is ours for the asking. We are invited, even commanded, to "pray unto the Father with all the energy of heart, that [we] may be filled with this love."[8]

As an example, I share an experience related by Sister Lanett Ho

Ching, currently serving with her husband, President Francis Ho Ching, who presides over the Samoa Apia Mission. Sister Ho Ching relates:

"Years ago, our young family moved to a tiny home in Laie, Hawaii. The carport of our home had been converted into a studio apartment, where a man named Jonathan lived. Jonathan had been our neighbor in another place. Feeling it wasn't a coincidence that the Lord had put us together, we decided to be more open about our activities and membership in the Church. Jonathan enjoyed our friendship and loved spending time with our family. He liked learning about the gospel, but he was not interested in committing to the Church.

"In time, Jonathan earned the nickname 'Uncle Jonathan' with our children. As our family continued to grow, so did Jonathan's interest in our happenings. Our invitations to holiday parties, birthdays, school events, and Church activities extended to family home evenings and the children's baptisms.

"One day I received a phone call from Jonathan. He needed help. He suffered from diabetes and had developed a severe foot infection that required an amputation. Our family and neighboring ward members walked him through that time of trial. We took turns at the hospital, and priesthood blessings were offered. While Jonathan was in rehab, with the help of Relief Society sisters, we cleaned his apartment. The priesthood brethren built a ramp to his doorway and hand railings in the bathroom. When Jonathan returned home, he was overcome with emotion.

"Jonathan began taking the missionary lessons again. The week before New Year's, he called me and asked, 'What are you doing on New Year's Eve?' I reminded him about our annual party. But instead, he replied, 'I want you to come to my baptism! I want to start this new year right.' After 20 years of 'come and see,' 'come and help,' and 'come and stay,' this precious soul was ready to be baptized.

"In 2018, when we were called to be mission president and companion, Jonathan's health was declining. We begged him to stay strong awaiting our return. He carried on for almost a year, but the

Lord was preparing him to come home. He passed away peacefully in April 2019. My daughters attended their 'Uncle Jonathan's' funeral and sang the same song we sang at his baptism."

I introduce the second requirement for successfully sharing the message of the Restoration with this question: what is it that will make your invitation appealing to someone? Isn't it you, the example of your life? Many who have heard and received the message of the Restoration were initially attracted by what they perceived in a member or members of the Church of Jesus Christ. It may have been the way they treated others, the things they said or didn't say, the steadiness they displayed in difficult situations, or simply their countenance.[9]

Whatever it may be, we cannot escape the fact that we need to understand and live the principles of the restored gospel as best we can for our invitations to be inviting. It is something often referred to today as authenticity. If the love of Christ dwells in us, others will know that our love for them is genuine. If the light of the Holy Spirit burns within us, it will rekindle the Light of Christ within them.[10] What you are lends authenticity to your invitation to come experience the joy of the fulness of the gospel of Jesus Christ.

The third requisite is liberal use of the instrument of conversion that God designed for this last gospel dispensation, the Book of Mormon. It is palpable evidence of Joseph Smith's prophetic calling and convincing evidence of the divinity and Resurrection of Jesus Christ. Its exposition of our Heavenly Father's plan of redemption is unequalled. When you share the Book of Mormon, you share the Restoration.

When Jason Olson was a teenager, he was warned repeatedly by family members and others against becoming a Christian. He had two good friends, however, who were members of The Church of Jesus Christ of Latter-day Saints, and they often discussed religion. His friends, Shea and Dave, respectfully countered arguments that others had given Jason against faith in Jesus Christ. Finally, they gave him a copy of the Book of Mormon, saying, "This book will answer your questions. Please read it." He reluctantly accepted the book and put it in his backpack, where it stayed for several months. He didn't want to leave it at home where his family might see it, and he didn't want to disappoint Shea and Dave by returning it. Finally, he settled on the solution of burning the book.

One night, with a lighter in one hand and the Book of Mormon in the other, he was about to set fire to the book when he heard a voice in his mind that said, "Do not burn my book." Startled, he paused. Then, thinking he had imagined the voice, he attempted again to ignite the lighter. Again, the voice came to his mind: "Go to your room and read my book." Jason put the lighter away, walked back to his bedroom, opened the Book of Mormon, and began to read. He continued day after day, often into the early hours of the morning. As Jason came to the end and prayed, he recorded, "I was filled from the crown of my head to the soles of my feet with the Spirit. . . . I felt full of light. . . . It was the most joyous experience I had ever had in my life." He sought baptism and later became a missionary himself.

Perhaps it goes without saying that despite genuine love and sincerity, many, if not most, of our invitations to share the message of the Restoration will be declined. But remember this: everyone is worthy of such an invitation—"all are alike unto God";[11] the Lord is pleased with every effort we make, no matter the outcome; a declined invitation is no reason for our association to end; and a lack of interest today may well turn to interest tomorrow. Regardless, our love remains constant.

Let us never forget that the Restoration has come out of intense ordeal and sacrifice. That is a subject for another day. Today we rejoice in the fruits of the Restoration, one of the most surpassing being the power once again to bind on earth and in heaven.[12] As expressed years ago by President Gordon B. Hinckley, "If nothing else came out of all of the sorrow and travail and pain of the restoration than the sealing power of the holy priesthood to bind together families forever, it would have been worth all that it has cost."[13]

The ultimate promise of the Restoration is redemption through Jesus Christ. The Resurrection of Jesus Christ is the proof that He, in fact, possesses power to redeem all who will come unto Him—redeem them from sorrow, injustice, regret, sin, and even death. Today is Palm Sunday; a week from today is Easter. We remember, we always remember, Christ's suffering and death to atone for our sins, and we celebrate that most wonderful of Sundays, the Lord's day, on which He rose from the dead. Because of the Resurrection of Jesus Christ, the Restoration has meaning, our mortal lives have meaning, and ultimately our very existence has meaning.

Joseph Smith, the great prophet of the Restoration, offers the overarching testimony for our time of the resurrected Christ: "That he lives! For we saw him, even on the right hand of God."[14] I humbly add my witness to Joseph's and to that of the apostles and prophets before him and the apostles and prophets who have succeeded him, that Jesus of Nazareth is the promised Messiah, the Only Begotten Son of God, and the resurrected Redeemer of all mankind.

"We testify that those who prayerfully study the message of the Restoration and act in faith will be blessed to gain their own witness of its divinity and of its purpose to prepare the world for the promised Second Coming of our Lord and Savior, Jesus Christ."[15] Christ's Resurrection makes His promises sure. In the name of Jesus Christ, amen.

Notes

1. Acts 3:21.
2. Ephesians 1:10.
3. James 1:5.
4. 2 Nephi 2:8.
5. David O. McKay, letter to Sarah M. Hilton, June 3, 1921, Church History Library, Salt Lake City.
6. John 1:46.
7. See 1 John 4:18.
8. Moroni 7:48.
9. President David O. McKay observed: "Every person who lives in this world wields an influence, whether for good or for evil. It is not what he says alone, it is not alone what he does. It is what he is. Every man, every person radiates what he or she is" (*Teachings of Presidents of the Church: David O. McKay* [2003], 227).
10. See John 1:9; Doctrine and Covenants 88:6–13; 93:2.
11. 2 Nephi 26:33.
12. See Matthew 16:19; 18:18; Doctrine and Covenants 110:14–16; 132:19, 46.
13. Gordon B. Hinckley, "As One Who Loves the Prophet," in Susan Easton Black and Charles D. Tate Jr., eds., *Joseph Smith: The Prophet, the Man* (1993), 6.
14. See Doctrine and Covenants 76:22–24.
15. "The Restoration of the Fulness of the Gospel of Jesus Christ: A Bicentennial Proclamation to the World," Apr. 5, 2020, in Russell M. Nelson, "Hear Him," *Ensign* or *Liahona*, May 2020, 91.

GO FORWARD IN FAITH

PRESIDENT RUSSELL M. NELSON
President of The Church of Jesus Christ of Latter-day Saints

My beloved brothers and sisters, as we come to the end of this historic conference, we express our gratitude to the Lord. The music has been sublime and the messages inspiring.

During this conference, we have experienced many highlights. On this bicentennial anniversary, we have introduced a proclamation to the world declaring the reality of the Restoration of the gospel of Jesus Christ in its fulness.

We commemorated the Restoration with the Hosanna Shout.

We unveiled a new symbol signifying our faith in the Lord Jesus Christ and for visual recognition of official Church information and materials.

We have called for a global day of fasting and prayer, that the present pandemic may be controlled, caregivers protected, the economy strengthened, and life normalized. This fast will be held on Good Friday, April 10. What a great Friday that will be!

Next Sunday is Easter Sunday, when we will again commemorate the Atonement and Resurrection of our Lord Jesus Christ. Because of His Atonement, His gift of resurrection will come to all who have ever lived. And His gift of eternal life will come to all who qualify by fidelity to ordinances and covenants made in His holy temples.

The many inspiring components of this April 2020 general conference—and the sacred week that we now begin—can be summarized by two divinely decreed words: "Hear Him."[1] We pray that your focus on Heavenly Father, who spoke those words, and on His Beloved Son, Jesus Christ, will loom largest in your memories of all that has transpired. We pray that you will begin anew *truly* to hear, hearken to, and heed the words of the Savior.[2] I promise that decreased fear and increased faith will follow.

Thank you for your desire to make your homes true sanctuaries of faith, where the Spirit of the Lord may dwell. Our gospel study curriculum, *Come, Follow Me,* will continue to bless your lives. Your consistent efforts in this endeavor—even during those moments when you feel that you are not being particularly successful—will change your life, that of your family, and the world. We will be strengthened as we become even more valiant disciples of the Lord, standing up and speaking up for Him, wherever we are.

Now, let's talk about temples. We have 168 dedicated temples across the world. Others are at various stages of planning and construction. When plans are announced to erect a new temple, it becomes part of our sacred history.

It may seem odd to announce new temples when all our temples are closed for a while.

More than a century ago, President Wilford Woodruff foresaw conditions such as ours today, as recorded in his dedicatory prayer of the Salt Lake Temple, given in 1893. Some of you may have recently seen excerpts from this remarkable prayer on social media.

Hear these pleadings from a mighty prophet of God: "When Thy people shall *not* have the opportunity of entering this holy house . . . and they are oppressed and in trouble, surrounded by difficulties . . . and shall turn their faces towards this Thy holy house and ask Thee for deliverance, for help, for Thy power to be extended in their behalf, we beseech Thee, to look down from Thy holy habitation in mercy . . . and listen to their cries. Or when the children of Thy people, in years to come, shall be separated, through any cause, from this place, . . . and they shall cry unto Thee from the depths of their affliction and sorrow to extend relief and deliverance to them, we humbly entreat Thee to . . . hearken to their cries, and grant unto them the blessings for which they ask."[3]

Brothers and sisters, during times of *our* distress when temples *are* closed, you can still draw upon the power of your temple covenants and endowment as you honor your covenants. Please use this time when temples are closed to continue to live a temple-worthy life or to become temple worthy.

Talk about the temple with your family and friends. Because Jesus Christ is at the center of everything we do in the temple, as you think more about the temple you will be thinking more about Him. Study and pray to learn more about the power and knowledge with which you have been endowed—or with which you will yet be endowed.

Today we are pleased to announce plans to construct eight new temples in the following locations: Bahía Blanca, Argentina; Tallahassee, Florida; Lubumbashi, Democratic Republic of the Congo; Pittsburgh, Pennsylvania; Benin City, Nigeria; Syracuse, Utah; Dubai, United Arab Emirates; and Shanghai, People's Republic of China.

In all eight locations, Church architects will work with local officials so that the temple will harmonize with and be a beautiful addition to each community.

The plan for a temple in Dubai comes in response to their gracious invitation, which we gratefully acknowledge.

Context for the plan for Shanghai is very important. For more than two decades, temple-worthy members in the People's Republic of China have attended the Hong Kong China Temple. But in July 2019, that temple was closed for long-planned and much-needed renovation.

In Shanghai, a modest multipurpose meeting place will provide a way for Chinese members to continue to participate in ordinances of the temple—in the People's Republic of China—for them and their ancestors.[4]

In every country, this Church teaches its members to honor, obey, and sustain the law.[5] We teach the importance of the family, of being good parents and exemplary citizens. Because we respect the laws and regulations of the People's Republic of China, the Church does *not* send proselyting missionaries there; nor will we do so now.

Expatriate and Chinese congregations will continue to meet separately. The Church's legal status there remains *unchanged*. In an initial phase of facility use, entry will be by appointment only. The Shanghai Temple will *not* be a temple for tourists from other countries.

These eight new temples will bless the lives of many people on both sides of the veil of death. Temples are a crowning part of the Restoration of the fulness of the gospel of Jesus Christ. In God's goodness and generosity, He is bringing the blessings of the temple closer to His children *everywhere*.

As the Restoration continues, I know that God will continue to reveal many great and important things pertaining to His kingdom here on earth.[6] That kingdom *is* The Church of Jesus Christ of Latter-day Saints.

Dear brothers and sisters, I express my love for you. During this time of tension and uncertainty, and invoking the authority vested in me, I would like to confer upon you an apostolic blessing.

I bless you with peace and increasing faith in the Lord.[7]

I bless you with a desire to repent and become a little more like Him each day.[8]

I bless you to know that the Prophet Joseph Smith is the prophet of the Restoration of the gospel of Jesus Christ in its fulness.

Should there be illness among you or your loved ones, I leave a blessing of healing, consistent with the will of the Lord.

I so bless you, adding once more my expression of love for each of you, in the sacred name of Jesus Christ, amen.

Notes

1. Joseph Smith—History 1:17; see also Luke 9:35.
2. See John 10:27; Revelation 3:20; Mosiah 26:21, 28; Doctrine and Covenants 29:7.
3. Wilford Woodruff, dedicatory prayer of the Salt Lake Temple, Apr. 6, 1893, ChurchofJesusChrist.org; emphasis added.
4. For thousands of years, the Chinese people have kept clan histories and genealogies. Traditional Chinese ceremonies show respect for their ancestors, such as the Qingming Festival (清明节). This year's Qingming Festival (清明节) was calendared for April 4–5.
5. See Articles of Faith 1:12.
6. See Articles of Faith 1:9.
7. See John 14:27.
8. See 3 Nephi 27:27.